S0-CCA-511

A Manual for Life

<u>Submit</u>
Object
death
Power

<u>Surrender</u>
Self
life
Strength

Erotic By Nature
David Steinberg, ed
Shakti Press, Red Alder Books
San Juan CA 1988

A Manual for Life

Bennet Wong and Jock McKeen

© 1992 B. Wong and J. McKeen

PD Seminars
Haven By-the-Sea
Site 9 - Davis Road
Gabriola Island, British Columbia, Canada V0R 1X0

Canadian Cataloguing in Publication Data

Wong, Bennet, 1930–
    A manual for life

        Includes bibliographical references and index.
        ISBN 0-9696755-0-X

        1. Life.   I. McKeen, Jock, 1946–   II. Title.
        BD431.M35 1992   128   C93-091022-2

Published under the auspices of the *Journal of Child and Youth Care*.

All rights reserved. No part of this work covered by the copyrights hereon may be reproduced or used in any form or by any means—graphic, electronic or mechanical—without the prior written permission of the publisher. Any request for photocopying, recording, taping or reproducing in information storage and retrieval systems of any part of this book shall be directed in writing to the Canadian Reprography Collective, 379 Adelaide Street West, Suite M1, Toronto, Ontario M5V 1S5.

Printed and bound in Canada by Hignell Printing Limited

 This book is printed on acid-free paper.

DEDICATION

For Reps
and Virginia Satir.
Your undaunted and wise spirits
continue to inspire us.

TABLE OF CONTENTS

Introduction

When I first became convinced that my survival depended upon my willingness and ability to make things right for others, I had no words or concepts that might account for this experience of infancy. Even now, I have only the faintest understanding of how these pre-verbal images were transformed into personal choices that drew me away from my thespian fantasies and carved out an uneasy career as a professional helper.

As a young student of psychology I was rebuked by my teachers for polluting their pristine rivers of knowledge with reflections of the "irrelevant" and seemingly chaotic experience of my own life. By the time I entered the hallowed halls of Graduate School, however, I had learned to rise above these undisciplined urges and join my fellow students in their relentless search for the truth about the nature of the organism. I entered practice wondering if these organisms would, in fact, conform to my newly acquired body of knowledge, while fearing the possibility that they might not respond to my carefully rehearsed interventions.

Fitting my clients with their "diagnostic" strait-jackets was relatively easy although it was painfully obvious that, once contained, I had no key with which to set them free. For the first year or so, I was quite prepared to accept that their apparent resistance to change was something to do with me and I applied myself diligently to mastering the tools of my trade. In later years I urged myself to believe that it was their own pathological obstinance that thwarted my efforts, but the strain of trying to fix other lives was becoming increasingly unbearable. By the time the humanistic movement was in full swing in the late sixties, I was ready to look at some alternative ways of meeting my needs and bolstering my struggling ego. Here was a new orientation with some new techniques. Again, I prepared myself to become the expert in my chosen field. I tried to fill my emptiness with more concepts and more words, and continued to maintain the illusion.

By the time I met Bennet Wong and Jock McKeen in 1985, I was barely hanging on. My role as a professional offered only the flimsiest veil of assurance and the "irrelevant and seemingly chaotic experience of my own life" was speaking back to me in a foreign tongue. Encouraged by my partner Judith, I participated in one of the programs offered by PD Seminars and, fighting my own resistant pathology, I slowly—very slowly—began the painful task of unravelling the chronicles of an unreflected life by coaxing myself into the experience of the moment. In this strange, and sometimes empty, place, an emerging sense of Self began to challenge the textbook beliefs of my Psychology.

Somewhere along the way, I had failed to grasp the simple empirical principle that the nature of phenomena change in accordance with the stance of the observer. Slowly it began to dawn on me that other lives could only be understood in relation to my own life and that I was using my quest for objectivity to obscure the totality of one side of the equation. It was obvious to me that Ben and Jock were not only exploring this other side but had thrown the doors of learning wide open by revealing one side to the other, first in their own relationship and then in their work with program participants. I had never witnessed or experienced anything like it before and my excitement, tempered by fears about what I might discover, challenged my courage to leap across the chasm. But Englishmen prefer to build bridges.

When Ben and Jock graciously agreed that I should write a book about them and their relationship, I had in mind that I could use their trestles to pick my way across and begin the search for my own wisdom. It was clear from the outset that this would be no true biographical or pure scientific enterprise and I marvelled at their willingness to have their lives projected through such a crude and contaminated filter. Despite their assurances that "truth" is an experiential reality, I harboured serious doubts about the integrity of my "investigation." Then it occurred to me that my fascination with the relationship of Bennet Wong and Jock McKeen could become a legitimate scientific enquiry, but only as long as I was prepared to examine my own experience in the process. Whatever the beliefs of my old academic mentors, I was obliged to explore the world of my own subjective experience.

I am now convinced that a true psychology must reach down into the core of the lived experience—from the unheralded moment of spiritual enlightenment to the habituated minutiae of daily life. From here, our most cherished and time-tested concepts must remain open and responsive to the raw experience of being. It is from this foundation that Wong and McKeen have carved out their own beliefs, using philosophy and theory only when these abstractions fit the data—"until further notice." It is for this reason that *A Manual For Life* represents a radical and unique contribution to the literature.

Philosophers of the phenomenological tradition certainly have stressed the primacy of subjective reality and many psychologists have attempted to speculate about the nature of the experiential world. But philosophy has generally remained cold and distant while humanistic psychology has failed to produce the necessary analytic methodologies. In both cases the issues have been reduced to untestable polemics designed to challenge the so-called "scientific tradition." Meanwhile, those who have constructed their "knowledge" from Newtonian physics and Cartesian dualism have continued to abstract the life from the very lives they purport to study. *A Manual For Life* neither negates nor embraces these positions.

In the work of their own lives, Wong and McKeen have simply moved beyond the tedious debates that have separated the various schools of thought. Through their courage to confront the "isness" of their own experience they have detached themselves from the closed world views of philosophical prescriptions and, in their commitment to the integrity of their own truth, they have avoided the "rightness" and "wrongness" of academic psychologizing. Above all, within their own relationship, they have created a living experimental laboratory with standards of discipline and rigour capable of intimidating even the most zealous scientist-practitioner.

For many years now, Bennet Wong and Jock McKeen have been sharing their work and their world with those who come to participate in their programs on Gabriola Island. Their respect for each individual experience, combined with the elegance of their methods, serves to create a place of learning in which the shared truth of individual lives generates a constant flow of living data. Over these years they have meticulously sifted through the grist of personal and collective experiences in the development of their own ideas about our place in the universal order. Up to this point, the intensity of their engagement in this process has left little time for writing but their decision to publish *A Manual For Life* represents an important step toward sharing some of these ideas with other students of life. Hopefully, it is only a beginning.

As Editor of the *Journal of Child and Youth Care* I was delighted to have had the opportunity to participate in this project. Having published a number of fine articles contributed by these authors, I jumped at the prospect of assisting in the publication of this volume and, like many Wong and McKeen watchers around the world, I have no hesitation in asking for more.

Gerry Fewster, Ph.D.

FOREWORD

In response to many requests, this manual was first prepared as a compilation of many of the papers we had written for different journals, newsletters, and other publications, along with several new articles. They afforded a glimpse of some of the basic concepts that we use in our work with PD Seminars at Haven By-the-Sea and in workshops we have given in North America and Southeast Asia.

The manual was not intended to be a comprehensive body of information. Rather, it summarized the ideas that are presented in the "Come Alive" workshops and the "Phase Programs." Those of you who have taken these will find the ideas familiar, and perhaps useful for review. We hope you will also discover some new meanings to the experiences you had in the workshops, strengthening any transformational process that you may have begun. Those of you who have not attended any workshops may find the information useful in your everyday life and relationships, helping you to arrive at some insights into your life choices and patterns. The articles have been written with all of you in mind.

This version of *A Manual For Life* is an updated extension of the original. Friends and clients have commented on, and we ourselves have recognized the density of the *Manual*'s contents. We had fully intended to expand it into a more readable, more anecdotal, more easily digestible book, with examples gleaned from our readers, and possibly some graphics. More and more, however, we heard from people who loved wrestling with our ideas and the ideas of others that we had included in our writing. They reported that they could digest only a few pages at a time, and certainly could never relax into a state of easy reading; but they appreciated that in a book, much as we ourselves have in the past.

People increasingly wrote from all parts of the world requesting permission to use parts of the *Manual* for their teaching: the condensed writing suited their purposes very well. Many people said that they were using the *Manual* in their personal lives as a stimulus for discussion (or argument, depending on the state of their relationship). Such people liked the opportunity to fill in the blanks of our ideas with their own, using ours only as a catalyst for their own thought. Those who took our seminars were able to see the ideas in practice, in their interactions with fellow participants. Finally, we were told that the *Manual* would be used as a reference book for some courses in child care and human development if it were published in a more finished form.

As a consequence, instead of rewriting the *Manual* to make it more readable and less dense, we set about editing what we had already written to give it more consistency and integrity. Then we proceeded to write more, as densely as before but filling in gaps in the continuity of thought. Thus, the volume of the original manuscript was increased by half as much again. Consequently, we regret that we cannot offer relief to those of you who have loyally and patiently waited in hopes of simplification; we seem to have replaced density with more density. We hope that stimulation will more than make up for the disappointment.

Out of the great morass of philosophical and psychological theories in which we all swim, we believe that we have been able to select and refine some very interesting and useful concepts. They have been tested by many of you during your very generous participation in our experiential workshops. By acting as evaluators you have contributed to the rapid growth of PD Seminars and Haven By-the-Sea. To you we dedicate this writing, and we hope that these words will be personally meaningful to you.

We extend our appreciation to our Haven colleagues and support staff, who have helped to create the loving environment that provides such an effective context for learning; our friends (particularly Gerry and Judith Fewster), who encouraged and supported our writing; our sons, Kevin, Randy, and Justin, who have become so engaged with their own individual goals in life in such a responsible and shared fashion; and last but not least, we appreciate each other for our unwavering dedication to our own relationship, which has elucidated so many of the concepts that we have attempted to explicate in our own personal way.

A FABLE

Once upon a time, the entire Universe was filled with unrestricted, free-flowing energy that danced joyously and chaotically in all directions in the Garden of Energy. For eons, the Universe enjoyed this existence, this freedom. However, since everything was so perfect and predictable, the Universe gradually began to feel a disquieting sense of boredom. Then, one day while at play, just for fun, it decided to create some beings. Separating out pieces of its own energy, it shaped and embodied one pattern of a being into a triangle, and another into a circle. These were colored with the pigments of the rainbow and were named "Triangulus" and "Circula" so that they could be easily identified. Although both of their energy flows remained connected to the source and thus to one another, the Universe allowed them unrestricted freedom to move, travel and play so that they all could enjoy life to its maximum. And so they did!

Triangulus and Circula enjoyed their existence together with one another and with the Universe, exploring all the nooks and crannies of the Garden of Energy that was bathed in a warm, glowing light. The sky, the earth and all beings in them which were connected to one another and to them were theirs to discover; what fun! Since the energy that flowed through Triangulus and Circula was the same energy that flowed through the Universe and all the other Beings therein, they felt no fear. Curiosity was their gift.

After eons of play, as all things became known to them, like their creator before themselves, Circula and Triangulus began to feel a sense of sameness that gradually grew into a disquieting sense of boredom. Wanting some unpredictability for spice, they developed a game of hide-and-go-seek which they played not only with one another but also with the Universe and all of the other Beings therein. What fun!

Over more eons of time, the playing of hide-and-go-seek became other than fun; it became compelling! As it became more competitive, they discovered that the hiding became more effective when their connection with one another and with All Beings was disrupted and hidden. Soon, they were experiencing more disconnection than connection, and each began to feel isolated and alone. Since they no longer knew what each other was thinking or doing, the game of hide-and-go-seek began to take on aspects of anxiety and desperation. The fun turned into fear and the business of life became *serious!*

Now no longer being able to depend upon the basic connection of the flow of energy between themselves and other Beings, Circula and Triangulus desperately developed means of *controlling* one another and the Universe. Each was unable to tolerate the dreadful sense of isolation that each felt *even when in the company of the other*! So each began to develop ways of manipulating, seducing and bargaining with the other; together they began to bend the Universe to their *will*, overcoming and destroying much of the rest of the Universe so that they could feel more *secure*. The more that they did this, the more they lost the connection of their energy with all else and the more *suspicious* they became of one another and the entire Universe. The light turned harsh and piercing.

As they looked across to one another and to the Universe, they now experienced a frightening *abyss* between them. Instead of returning to their roots where their energy is already connected (although forgotten), they focused their energy upon building bridges across that chasm in order to contact one another. Such bridges included social skills, fantasy diversions, religions, scientific discoveries, new and better ways of communication and transportation, and groupings into common languages, families and couples. All of these were jealously protected, for fear of losing advantage and control over one another. Out of this fear grew experiences of jealousy, hurt feelings and ultimately, vengeance and violence. The Universe felt sad!

In spite of all of this, there remained a concern for one another since at root, they *were* one another! Not being able to feel the flow of energy connecting them, they instead began to make connections at a more superficial level. Instead of feeling *at one* with one another, when they were not competing, they began to feel a sense of *sympathy* and *empathy* for others; they developed a desire to *take care of* one another. In such a way, they managed to maintain *control* of their relationships, and began to feel *secure* again. Institutions and religions were developed around such a *morality*, and smugness and pride in *righteousness* were natural outcomes.

Now, across the great abyss, Triangulus and Circula expressed to one another their great *need* for one another, and each swore to take care of the other. Of course, what they had forgotten, and what they had lost was the fact that each of them was *already whole* and *already connected* to one another. So the belief in needing one another was a Big Lie. However, since they were able to dress up the Big Lie with hearts and flowers, they made it very appealing indeed, calling it their "Romance"! Now, they wanted each other to swear allegiance *for life,* even though by doing so they were committing themselves for a death of their own individual selves. The price that they had to pay was the sacrifice of their own personal potential of being! However, that did not matter to them, because to swear allegiance and to *submit* to the control of the other was exciting and full of the promise of security. Now, they did not have to stare across the big abyss. Rather, they spent their time in the movie house and fun palaces that made them forget about

Reality! They could spend their time *taking care of* one another instead of having to *care about* one another. Although they no longer could feel their connection with one another, they worked hard to get to know one another so that they could *please* one another.

In fact, what Circula and Triangulus now felt for one another was the certainty of *possessiveness* and *control*. For a long time, that did not matter—at least not until the control stopped working! Whether due to natural aging, or loss of roles, or the falling out of Romance by one of the people involved, the stark realism of being alone tended to leak out. When that happened to either Circula or Triangulus, each would feel the *pain* of loneliness. Being too difficult to bear, they converted that pain into *hurt feelings* and *anger* and each began to *blame* the other. This maneuver was a last ditch stand to prevent the self from falling into the abyss. So long as the other was to blame, this generated energy of anger provided a temporary sense of meaning to an otherwise horrifying experience of nothingness and depression. Out of this tendency to blame arose a whole new approach to life—becoming a *victim* in which the *other* became responsible for the self! Now life became not only serious, it became irresponsible!

Gradually, the institutions took over the responsibility for everybody, leaving each person only the right to do what was *politically correct*. To make life more predictable, Triangulus and Circula were forbidden to look triangular and circular; each was made to look like a grey box. Spontaneity, individuality and personal freedom became a thing of the past! The light of the Universe dimmed in the Garden of Energy as all movement, sound and color became legislated.

However, Circula and Triangulus, trapped in their politically correct grey box, yearned to return to their original shapes and colors—to be themselves! When they saw each other's personal pain, they felt sorry for one another and wanted to *help* one another. Realizing the original trap of wanting to take care of one another, they refused to do that any longer; they knew that they could not take away the other's pain. Instead, they learned how to be *responsible* for their own pain, to be *present* to witness the pain of the other, to *share* rather than blame. While so doing, they began to feel the connection of their energy at their roots, discovering that their hurt was the pain of their separation. When feeling their connection, they knew that each of their pain was one another's pain—that it was not just similar, it was the same! Now, they were able to *resonate* with one another's feelings, and no longer felt alone.

With that resonance, color and aliveness returned to the lives of all Beings. The Garden of Energy began to flower and flow freely again. For Triangulus and Circula, life again became free, full of light and movement. They danced and sang, played and worked with full hearts. And the Universe smiled!

THE BEGINNING

Waiting at the Station

Most people seem to believe that destiny has some particular goal for them, that they were meant to become something special. To such persons, the task in life is to discover exactly what that goal is, to figure out the destination before being prepared to commit time and effort to getting there. This is a common life-stance among adolescents, who believe that education is a waste of time until they decide on an occupational goal. Many people live much of their lives in this immature pattern, whiling their time away until they know their exact destination.

In effect, such people believe that there is a specific train that will carry them to a particular locus of success; so they wait in the train station watching all the trains (opportunities) go by, entertaining themselves at the computer games with all the other waiting people. They might closely examine each passing train to see if it is the right one, but because the destinations are never clearly marked, each train passes without being boarded.

In the station, these waiting people become restless and discontent, wondering when they will be given specific instructions about which train to catch. Even when they are advised to board a specific train, they find fault and raise doubts rather than taking the risk of embarking. They are afraid of wasting time by getting on the wrong train—they fear that they might arrive at a wrong destination and then have to return to this station to catch the right train. So trains keep passing them by. Yet they do nothing but waste time in the train station.

What such people do not realize is that *all* of the trains have the same destination—death. They may have different itineraries, with different stop-offs en route (e.g., a different career), but ultimately, the terminus is the same. That being the case, these people would do well to board the very next train, take the first opportunity to become involved with the activities on the train, and be present for the trip. If they were to do so, they would notice their fellow travellers, the ever-changing passing scenery, and the pleasure of the motion of the train. While on the train, their challenge would be to discover creative uses of time and talents, especially in relationship to the other passengers.

An important element in selecting a train to board would be the character of the passengers already on board. Are they serious minded or revellers, musicians or poets, relaxed or tense, morally righteous or libertarians? These qualities will give some clue to the atmosphere that might be expected on a prolonged journey.

Giving up the investment in the future goal allows a person to enjoy the journey in the present. At any of the stop-offs, it is possible to get off a particular train and board another. The danger in disembarking is that one might once again get stuck in the waiting room of another train station—to become uninvolved, instead of throwing oneself onto another passing train, to have yet another new experience!

A Model for Communication

CONTEXT (BACKGROUND)

Each time you enter a new situation, you carry with you a context that is based upon your past experience (both recent and more distant). So you do not enter new situations fresh; you color them in terms of other experiences you have had. For example, if you have been having a bad day and feel irritable, when you meet a new person you will begin your interaction in an irritable frame of mind. On the other hand, if you have been feeling buoyant and happy and then enter a difficult situation, you will begin in a positive frame of mind.

The context is the *background* or *substrate* against which immediate situations are viewed. Thus, one can benefit from a periodic checking with one's internal world to see what the context is. One should not take the context for granted, as it can shift and change. A moment of closed-eyes investigation of thoughts and feelings will give you an impression of the background you bring in. As you observe your thoughts and note your feelings, you will find what might be seen as trivial experiences—repetitive thoughts, or a vague mood that doesn't seem to have any origin. Note these—they will be coloring the situations you enter. Indeed, the context will even help select, out of the infinite variety of possible perceptions, those that you will notice.

PERCEPTION (FIVE SENSES)

As you open your eyes to observe another person, you will begin to absorb information about that person. If you do not attempt to communicate, but instead permit the impressions of the other to wash over you, you will develop a "soft eyes" impression of the other. You can appreciate the other as you would a fine sculpture in a museum. In a matter of seconds you will take in thousands of items of information through your senses—seeing, hearing, smelling, tasting, and touch. Although most of this is done subconsciously, you *do* quickly take in this vast array of data. What is interesting is that none of these thousands of pieces of information means anything—they are simply the result of stimulation of your nervous system. They are experienced by your brain as raw sensory information—shape, colour, texture, smells, and sounds.

Note that these are *impressions*—a hint of a fragrance, a subtle sound, a shading of expression on the face of the other. The perceptions do not mean anything in themselves; in order to make our world understandable, we go to work subconsciously on each of these thousands of pieces of information to *make them mean something*—we perform the mental operation of interpreting. The perceptions are sensory; the interpretations are the mental operations that provide the meaning.

INTERPRETATION (MEANING ATTRIBUTION)

As you observe your partner, you will have impressions of the way he/she is sitting; the color of skin; the position of hands; the color and type of clothing, jewellery, skin tone, hair style; and countless other features. From these impressions, you will assemble an overall picture, which you interpret. Now, it is important to realize that your interpretations are not correct—they are a *best-guess* at the meaning of what you are witnessing. These interpretations assist you in making intelligible the huge amount of information that you have received from your senses. Although the interpretations are not correct, they are also never wrong. They are simply your way of making sense of the information you have.

One should always check with the other person, seeking agreement or disagreement relating to each interpretation. It is impossible to be either correct or wrong; nevertheless, I can check to see if my version of you matches your version of yourself. Note that if you agree with me, I am not right; we simply *agree*. If your opinion differs, I am not wrong; we simply *disagree*. When there is a difference in an interpretation, we do not have to agree; instead, we can become *curious* about the different viewpoints we have, and learn more about ourselves and each other. This attitude of curiosity with no right or wrong permits an openness to ongoing learning; to become fixated on who is right or wrong brings learning to a halt.

Common phrases to express your interpretations are:
- "I *interpret* that you are a kind person."
- "I *believe* that you are being honest."
- "I *think* that you are shy."
- "I *assume* that this is difficult for you."
- "I *imagine* that you are uncomfortable."
- "I *judge* that you are trying very hard to communicate."
- "I *speculate* that you are thinking of something else."
- "I *fantasize* that you are feeling very young."

Interpreting is a mental operation that involves thinking. A common mistake is to confuse interpretations with feelings. Thus the phrase "I feel that you are . . ." is *never* a feeling; instead, it is a misrepresentation of "I think that you are . . ." Many people are afraid to express their interpretations because the idea of judging someone else has taken on negative overtones. Yet judging (interpreting) is merely your way of making sense of information in order for you to more profoundly know another person. Judgment does not necessarily imply a rejection; indeed, pure judgment simply involves drawing distinctions in order to make sense of random data. It is from these interpretations that all your feelings come: how you interpret the data of your senses will determine whether you wish to move toward or away from another person.

FEELING

Based on the interpretations you make, you will develop your feelings. Feelings are experiences in the body involving changes in blood flow and energy shifts. There are basically two kinds of feelings—positive and negative.

Positive feelings involve an opening up of the blood vessels in the body, and are associated with a sensation of warmth and well-being. When you sense this positive feeling, you will feel like moving toward the other. You would express a positive feeling in these ways: " I like you," "I am drawn to you," "I am attracted to you," "I feel comfortable with you," "I feel close to you," "I feel warm with you," "I love you." The overall experience is one of feeling close and comfortable and wanting to move toward the other.

Negative feelings involve a contraction of the blood vessels in the body, with an accompanying feeling of tightness, discomfort, and coolness and a desire to move back. You might express a negative feeling in any of these ways: "I am uncomfortable with you," "I dislike you," "I feel distant from you," "I am repulsed by you," "I don't like you," "I am afraid of you," "I hate you," "I feel like moving away from you." The overall experience is one of feeling distant, cool, and repelled.

Note that a negative feeling does not imply that the other person is bad or wrong; it simply reflects a judgment within the person who has the negative feeling, who for some reason experiences a desire to move away. For example, when you chose your outfit this morning, you were negative to all the other clothes in your closet; when you choose chocolate ice cream, you are negative to all the other flavors that you could have chosen. So, negative and positive feelings involve *choice* and *valuing*; they do not say anything about the worth of the other person, but rather speak of the valuing process within the person having the feelings.

Also, be aware that the feelings you have are entirely based upon your context and interpretations. The same perceptions can be colored differently given different contexts and interpretations, and it is possible to feel either positively or negatively about any perception. For example, the sight of a big man with a knife could be interpreted in various ways. If one were to interpret the man as a threatening killer, one would likely have a negative feeling and draw away; if instead one were to interpret him as a chef who is about to carve a roast of beef, one might draw close to get the first piece! The feelings are determined by the interpretations of the perceptions.

Context
(Background)

Perceptions:
(Five senses) *I see, hear, taste, smell, touch*
Interpretations: *I believe, think, assume, interpret,*
(Meanings) *imagine, fantasize, judge, speculate*

> NOTE: NOBODY IS EVER RIGHT OR WRONG . . .
> . . .YOU CAN ONLY AGREE OR DISAGREE.
> **CHECK** IT OUT!

Feelings: POSITIVE—*like, love, open, warm, attracted, comfortable,*
move toward
NEGATIVE—*dislike, hate, closed, cool, repulsed,*
uncomfortable, move away
Intention: *What I feel like doing, intend to do, want to do, will do*
Action: *What I do*

INTENTION

Intention involves the will in translating your feelings into action. For each perception/interpretation/feeling complex, it is possible to develop an intention about what you would like to do in response. You do not ever have to follow a feeling; human beings have free will, and can decide to act in opposition to their feelings. For example, you might feel attracted to someone, and decide not to pursue this attraction because of commitment to an established relationship. In a similar manner, you might be afraid of someone and decide to approach that person to talk about your fear, instead of withdrawing and following the feeling. You can always learn about yourself from a situation, whether you follow your feeling or not.

Also, you should always be ready in a dialogue to ask of the other, "What is your intention in telling me this?" This question raises a dialogue from a mundane interchange of ideas to the level of the deeper meanings involved in the communication. For example, if someone's intention were to express anger in order to clear the air and become closer to you, you might be interested in staying to face the anger; on the other hand, if that person's intention was simply to try to intimidate or get control of you, you might not want to stay engaged with the other. Clarifying your intentions can allow the communication to proceed to ever deeper levels.

ACTION

Once you become clear about your perceptions, interpretations, feelings, and intentions, any decisions to act will be uncomplicated, easily understood by others, and more effectively executed. With this kind of mastery and the development of increasing amounts of self-responsibility, your inner strength will grow. More and more, you will recognize how you are constantly creating your own reality. Then the possibilities for personal growth, expansion and transformation are limitless!

I've had the joy of others experiencing my pain
Been held, told by strangers that I am loved.
I've searched my soul, experienced my anger and sorrow.
I feel whole and yet there remains a void that needs to be filled
The fullness that only comes from experiencing the special love
And intimacy of one human being caring for another.
It is now easy to write and speak of love.
Even if it be in the abstract and uncommitted to a single soul.

I reached out my arms and cradled people who, hitherto I would
 have felt unwarranted of my time.
I've heard the screams of hurt; sobbed and felt their pain and my own.
I've come alive with the realization that life has its origins
 in the interconnectings of the human spirit
And when we become alone and unwilling to reach out and share
 that spirit,
We have allowed ourselves to die.
My fortune is that I am me. My salvation is that there was you.

—Larry Gold

CONSTRUCTIVISM

Constructivism is an epistemology[1] that proposes that all of our ideas about reality (our knowledge and belief systems) are *interpretations* of immediate experience. As such, we must continually refer our ideas back to *experience-as-a-whole* for verification and refinement. Most of this interpretation of reality is done through the use of *symbols*. The roots of such an approach can be found as far back as the writings of Kant, but more recently in the *phenomenology* of Husserl and the *pragmatism* of William James and John Dewey. Rollo May and Abraham Maslow did much to integrate phenomenology into humanistic psychology (as had gestalt psychology) through the synthesis of existential philosophy and psychiatry. Their main point was that *experience* is the most important source of data for psychology, at least equal (if not greater) in importance than data collected through *observation* (as proposed by the scientific methods).

Over recent years, the constructivist approach has been explored and applied to achieve insights into the individual, the family, and groups. The critical insight is that symbols are used to interpret and understand natural, social, and psychological worlds. It is important to recognize that

1.   these symbols themselves *are* the *psychological* world;
2.   these symbols *create* or *constellate* the *social* world; and
3.   these symbols *systematically influence* and *destabilize* the *natural* world.

The existentialists challenged the concept that "essence precedes existence," replacing it with Sartre's epigram that "existence precedes essence." The constructivists now propose that "epistemology precedes ontology" (the theory of the nature of being or reality). This opens the door to the possibility of innumerable "multiple realities" and "realms of being": there is then no absolute, correct reality, and each person, organization, or group can construct a unique version of reality with some possible underlying common themes (as with Jung's theory of archetypes).

Howard Gardner suggested that humans attempt to organize their understanding of reality through the use of their *multiple intelligences,* of which there are at least six:

1.   Logical-mathematical: the use of symbols and their relationships to one another

2.   Linguistic: the use of language
3.   Musical: the use of sounds in relationship with one another (as in melody)
4.   Spatial: the experience of locating the Self in relation to space
5.   Bodily-kinesthetic: the locations of inner experience
6.   Personal: the feelings and experiences unique to the person[2]

For the past four centuries, scientific philosophy has dominated our exploration of reality, reaching the zenith of its influence on society in the last century. Great strides in knowledge have been accomplished through the use of the logical-mathematical intelligence, with its emphasis on pure *observation* and *objectivity*. Although the study of human behavior did not readily lend itself to such a scientific approach, behavioral scientists struggled to force a fit in their desire to gain acceptability and credibility with their scientific colleagues. Rebelling against such an unnatural fit, the existentialists had a strong influence in establishing the view that *experience* is as important as *observation* in our understanding of human nature. Such a revolutionary idea struck home in the hearts of psychologists who were searching for the human element in their understanding of the person. The rising influence of humanistic psychology reflects such an awareness.

Early concepts that gained influence in the field recognized the importance of language in shaping reality. With its scientific inheritance, neurolinguistic programming (NLP) developed as one of many systems that attempted to break out of a narrow view of human behavior, returning to the individual the possibility of constructing a personal experience and reality. In the past two decades there has been an upsurge of a great variety of approaches to understanding human experience, most of which were unscientific and nonlogical and thus met with resistance from traditional bodies of psychology. The increasing influence of constructivism was seen to be a threat against the social order (e.g., to anticipate later chapters, "creation-centered spirituality" threatened the traditional Christian church and "holistic health" threatened the traditional medical model).

Accompanying and closely identified with the constructivist influence were the ideas of *structuralism,* which proposed that human experience was *structured* by deep, underlying patterns of behavior that are always pressuring for expression. Such an idea is not new, being readily seen in the philosophy of acupuncture and traditional Chinese medicine in ancient China. A resurgence of interest in Jung's ideas about myths and archetypes reflects these same ideas, none of which are very scientific. Despite the opposition of traditionalists, these approaches are becoming increasingly popular.

The humanistic approaches took considerable interest in bodily approaches to understanding human behavior. Reichian concepts and their many offshoots (e.g., bioenergetics, Feldenkrais and Alexander techniques, rolfing) expanded awareness of the bodily-kinesthetic and spatial elements involved in understanding and appreciating the world as it is created by human experience. Much work still needs to be done to understand more fully the language of the body. From a holistic health perspective, it is postulated about symptoms that *"the body speaks what the voice cannot."*

The significance of music in constructivist theory has yet to be fully studied, even though music obviously has considerable influence on human emotions, and is in turn affected by them. Musical styles and structures vary from one society to another; according to body approaches, cultural differences are held in the deep tissue. The patterns of these holdings are expressed in the unique music of that culture. In turn, these musical expressions influence the deep patterns of that culture.

Ultimately, it is the personal and unique use of all of these intelligences that matters. Each person moves in a social structure that imposes its mark (its commonly accepted version of reality) upon the individual. The commonly accepted version held today is still very scientific. When a person's experience of reality is in opposition to the official view, that individual has to decide either to abandon this personal perspective (the commonest solution) or to develop ways of surviving while remaining out of step with the rest of society. The more accepting the society is, the easier it is for the individual to own and share differing or multiple realities. Because such acceptance is not usual, the individual often finds it difficult to maintain a unique version of reality, let alone be able to share it. Yet such sharing in relationship to others is what would help the individual to discover and accept the Self.

> **Listen**
> Rest in the sombre shadows
> The quiet inner voice
> has been talking to you all your life
>
> Now you begin to listen
> —and the world opens
>
> Flooding with images
> from behind the dam
> of social propriety
>
> Accompanied by strange
> and haunting melodies
>
> —Jock McKeen

Notes

1. "A theory of the method or grounds of knowledge," The Concise Oxford Dictionary, 5th ed. (Oxford: Oxford University Press, 1967), 325.
2. H. Gardner, *Frames of Mind, The Theory of Multiple Intelligence* (New York: Basic Books, 1985).

Recommended Reading

Maslow, A.H. *The Psychology of Science: A Reconnaissance.* New York: Harper and Row, 1966.

May, R. and H.F. Ellenberger, eds. *Existence.* New York: Basic Books, 1958.

THE IDEAL SELF: STRIVING FOR PERFECTION

It is remarkable how often individuals are self-critical and self-deprecatory. Such persons have a low sense of self-esteem and are unhappy with their accomplishments, no matter how good they may be in the eyes of others. By society's yardstick, many such people are very successful, occupying positions of power and authority. In their personal lives they may appear to have loving families and many important and good friends. However, within themselves they are unhappy, often depressed, with feelings of emptiness, meaninglessness, and guilt. They work hard, achieve much, and are good at what they do, but *it is never enough.*

Frequently, the history of these people includes what society would describe as an ideal family; some in actuality could be described as *dysfunctional.* Their parents are often seen to be authoritarian or perfectionistic, with great demands for achievement being placed on the children. Sometimes, however, the parents are seen to be quite the opposite in terms of *outward* expectations. They may be quite liberal and accepting of their children, but they themselves usually have achieved much and have lived exemplary lives filled with success. The unspoken injunction would be to "be perfect!" Even if that injunction is absent, the obvious signs of their success have established a base level against which the children compare themselves and find themselves wanting. Sometimes, the background history is one of poverty or family neglect; children from these backgrounds may have reacted by vowing to rise above their family's state of helplessness by striving for achievement and power.

A general assumption is that each one of us is born with an "Authentic Self." This would be the basic nature and characteristic personality of the infant. As every mother of many children will attest, even from the earliest days of life each child has a unique and individual quality, a particular essence of the individual's being (some refer to this as the "soul"). This includes all the potential of that person's being that could come to fruition with time and future experience.

It is easy to imagine how the newborn child must feel when being held, cared for, fed, and played with. The parents' attitudes toward the child are being transmitted during all of these interactive activities. Their feelings will have considerable effect on the degree to which the child will experience the world as a safe and accepting place; such feelings can range from being ecstatic over having the child to resenting the added burden. Most often, it is a combination of both extremes, shifting from time to time and dependent on the circumstances.

At some level, no matter how great the intent to be otherwise, each parent has expectations of the newborn. (We have known people to have suffered from a life-long parental injunction that all they wanted was for their child *to be happy.*) The child will have to contend with all of those expectations. Somewhere in the depths of the developing personality, each individual will become aware that behavior must be modified to please the parents. This is the normal course of events as a child matures. Through daily experience, children form an image of how they must be in order to please those upon whom they are entirely dependent for survival. That developing image of the Self that will be acceptable and will gain approval (and thus ensure survival) is referred to as the "Ideal Self." The expectations, demands, and injunctions become codified, memorized, and incorporated into a *self-regulating system of behavior* in the maturing person. Thus, children are caught in an early bind. What they want to do, to express the impulses of the Authentic Self, is most often in opposition to what is expected by the parents (and later by all authorities, institutions, and society in general). As those expectations become incorporated within the personality as a self-governing Ideal Self, the struggle becomes an inner one within the Self. It occurs even in the absence of the parents or any external authority.

In most cases, the *desires* of the Authentic Self must be surrendered to the Ideal Self's *demands* for acceptance. The result is usually some form of *compromise* that establishes the expressed behavior of a developing "Actual Self." Through such a process, the growing child becomes a relatively well-behaved, disciplined, civilized person prepared to be educated for responsibilities as a future adult. Each of us lives with these three selves, trying to please all of them in order to maintain some emotional balance and ease (that is, "sanity").

From the outside, the emerging struggle between the parts of the Self appears relatively peaceful. The child is seen to be merely "growing up" and "maturing" into a "good" child, a "cooperative" student, and a "responsible" citizen. The compromises being made are not unreasonable; they are for the child's "good." Unfortunately, every time that the Authentic Self is abandoned in an effort to behave more like the Ideal Self, the Self recognizes that abandonment and reacts with *self-hatred.* Thus, even though that person achieves a great deal, much of the Self is denied.

The "Path of Glory"
—and Back!

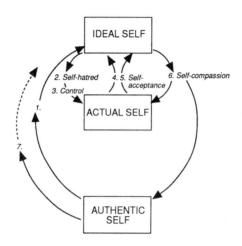

1. The child tries to please the parent by striving to become the Ideal Self.
2. Abandonment of the Authentic Self produces self-hatred.
3. The Actual Self establishes *control* in the real world.
4. Recognizing that it has fallen short of expectations, the Actual Self strives toward greater perfection, abandoning the Authentic Self even more, thus generating even more self-hatred and establishing a *self-hating cycle*.
5. By becoming *aware* of the Ideal Self, the Actual Self can begin to *accept* the totality of the Self, feeling *compassion* and understanding for having had to compromise so much in the past.
6. This *self-compassion* leads to an acceptance of all parts of the Self, including the part that has found it necessary to abandon its Authentic Self in the face of reality. This leads to a greater awareness of the whole Self, including the Authentic Self.
7. The cycle begins all over again.

The result is a growing accumulation of self-hatred that can be felt as feelings of anxiety and depression or witnessed in compulsively self-destructive behavior. Patterns of self-defeating behavior with resulting low self-esteem are thus established, even as the person is driven to greater heights of achievement, with ever-increasing amounts of self-hatred. Evidence of being trapped in this cycle will be seen at all levels of these people's beings. Emotionally, they might experience anxiety or depression. More often, in order *not* to feel the emotional discomforts related to self-hatred, they develop any number of obsessive or compulsive behaviors or other signs of neurotic maladaptation. Physically, a wide variety of symptoms of illness can develop. Spiritually, an emptiness (anomie) might be experienced, or a lack of direction in life or deep sense of guilt.

In our society, it is these very driven and achieving people that ultimately arrive at the "top" to become our political and economic leaders, many of them filled with self-hatred and anger. Their choices are simple: they can go for more power and achievement (and hate themselves even more), they can somatize their anger and become physically ill, they can manifest self-destructive behavior (such as failure, addictions of all sorts, or family disorders), or they can direct their anger outward in the form of blame or aggression. Because of the power that people generally invest in such leaders, how they handle this self-hatred has many consequences for society! Wars, social unrest, antisocial behavior, addictive disorders, and family dysfunctions are a few of the possible symptoms.

To break this cycle of striving for perfection, where much is achieved but a load of self-hatred is generated and accumulates, each person must learn about self-compassion. The first step is to become aware of these patterns of striving, accepting the Self for doing the best that it can under the circumstances. The next step is to acknowledge the patterns, to others as well as to oneself; this acknowledgement overcomes the fixed pattern of denial, and frees up the fixation. In this revealing of the Self, acceptance is demonstrated and furthered. We call these the *three A's of self-compassion: awareness, acknowledgement*, and *acceptance*. Even the struggle toward perfection must be accepted, though not necessarily acted upon. Through this acceptance, the person can develop a growing pattern of self-compassion. When that occurs, the repetitive pattern will be altered and transformed, slowly at first, but becoming increasingly familiar and acceptable to the Self.

Through self-awareness, people notice the patterns of achievement and desires for perfection, which mask their underlying feelings of helplessness, inadequacy, and inferiority. With some warmth and possible amusement ("Here I go again!"), such persons can recognize the persistence of the pattern. At this point, they have a wide variety of possible reactions:

1. They can deny the patterns, or forget about them, and continue with the cycle with all of its accompanying emotional, physical, and spiritual consequences. This is the "Path Of Glory" (see figure).

2. They can fall into despair or self-pity for having to contend with the inevitability and hopelessness of the situation, developing feelings of depression and anxiety. This is the "Path Of Helplessness."

3. They can focus on blaming others (like parents and other authorities) for their having contributed to the creation of this dilemma, becoming obsessed with revenge and retribution. This will lead the person to become stuck with such patterns of behavior, with an accompanying accumulation of inner rage and all of its dire consequences to the body and mind. This is the "Path Of Blame."

4.   They can accept themselves for the kinds of persons they are and realize that they have a choice to act or not act on the impulse toward perfection. They may choose to love themselves, to take it easy for a change and pay some attention to their needs for relaxation or pleasure. This is the "Path Of Self-Compassion."

What must be realized is that we will always have our three inner selves, caught in the dilemma of striving for perfection and generating self-hatred. It is useless to try to deny our Ideal Self. That only serves to add to our struggle by creating the goal to be more of the Authentic Self, which becomes another Ideal Self with even more possibilities of generating self-hatred.

All parts of the Self need to be accepted. We must come to know the Ideal Self, acknowledging and honoring it; nevertheless, we do not have to respond to it. All of the feelings accompanying this awareness can be felt and then cycled through to new patterns of behavior and feelings. Then the cycle of self-hatred will be broken, and the maturation process can proceed.

Recommended Reading

Rubin, T. *Compassion and Self-Hate*. New York: Macmillan, 1985.

Horney, K. *Neurosis and Human Growth*. New York: W.W. Norton and Co., 1950.

Is Change Possible?

INTRODUCTION

Can a leopard change its spots, or a tiger lose its stripes? The advent of the human potential movement ushered in an era of hope for the overcoming of human shortcomings and woes. Since the proliferation of growth programs that began in the sixties, there has been an unspoken assumption that change is possible and that the possibilities of the human being are virtually limitless. The underlying theme seems to be that one does not have to tolerate personal or situational limitations: life is what you make of it, and we are totally responsible for everything that happens to us. If you don't like your life the way it is, you simply need to "get off your position" and create a new life more to your taste. In short, you are in the driver's seat, and the possibilities are limited only by your aspirations, your desire for change, and your willingness to go for it.

THE MORALITY OF IDEALISM

The recipe for this way of living includes a liberal dose of *moralism*. Everything is seen in terms of right and wrong, or worse and better, or greater and lesser. In short, it's not okay today/here/now/with me; however, it *could be okay* tomorrow/there/then/with a better me. Life today is not good; tomorrow will be better. I am not very realized today; I hope I will become something greater in the future.

This perspective has led to a great deal of idealistic goal setting and personal ambition to change oneself or one's situation. How often have you said such things as "I need to change my life (work, partner)" or "when I finally accomplish this, then I'll be happier" or "when I finally achieve this, then everything will be great." The basic theme is that *things are not okay as they are* and that there is a better day coming in the future, after the necessary changes are made to create a richer life. Often, a deep-seated depression accompanies this attitude, assuming that things are not okay as they are. Along with the depression comes an ambitious drive to change oneself, one's life, or one's situation, in order to approach the desired changed condition. Many believe that with enough effort and attention, one can even restructure one's personality, eradicating bothersome traits and giving birth to brand new ones. Generally, this thrust to change is accompanied by guilt and despair as one does not match up to one's aspirations.

TRANSCENDENCE

Another interpretation of change involves an attitude that one can "transcend"—literally rise above one's circumstances and deal with it all from another plane. If life is bothersome, just ignore the troubling aspects and move beyond them. For those who adopt this frame of reference, there often is a floating feeling of blissful detachment. However, this approach operates against living participation. The Self is detached from the world and other humans. Hence, one leaves life without having fully entered it.

DEVALUING THE SELF

The attempt to change oneself through idealism and striving into something better is generally accompanied by a continual devaluing of the Self. In all the years that we have worked with people, we have always found this attitude to be counterproductive to personal development. The harder one tries to get away from one's situation, the more stuck and fixated one becomes. The mechanistic "change me" perspective and the idealism and hope of a better tomorrow operate against full participation in a life in the present. The goals of idealism kill present circumstances and interfere with the organic development of events. Craving for improvement interferes with the expansion of the present into a vigorous future. One becomes fixated in the attempt to escape from where one is. One affirms an image, a simulacrum of how things could be, and hence fails to exist fully. The pursuit of the illusion of change contributes to one's nonbeing.

We propose an alternative: to courageously resist the dissatisfaction of the achievement ethic, and *affirm the substance of one's life* in the present, thus contributing to the unfolding of one's beingness. Rather than focusing on an unreal image, we emphasize facing the facts of the living present, accepting one's beingness, and moving from here.

THE RADICAL HYPOTHESIS

Our hypothesis is this: *change is not possible.* It is pointless to try to change one's given biological structure or one's basic personality. If you were born a woman, then a woman you will be. You cannot eradicate your life history by forcing yourself to ignore it. Everybody is dealt a hand in life; most people are afraid to play their hand or get mired in resentments over not receiving better cards. Wouldn't it be better to play it out as best we can, even with insufficient advice and information along the way?

We have found that this attitude frightens many. There is a certain security in getting ready for the future, which will be better. If one drops the idea of there being future possibilities at all, and directly focuses on one's life as it is, a rush of fear floods one: Is this all there is? Is there no salvation from my lot? At least when I am sick, or in need of change, then as a patient I believe that I know who I am, know what to expect of myself and others, and I have a certain sense of security in this. If I don't have this definition of myself, then who am I?

We assume that the structure of the personality is largely set from the early days of one's life. One inherits traits, and these are affected by the young child's experience. By the time the individual is only months old, the basic personality pattern has been fixed in quite a profound way. This *deep structure*, which is an amalgam of inherited tendencies, early experiences, and learning, will persist for the lifetime of the individual. The deep structure is not a thing, and it is not anatomically located; rather, it is formed of the interrelationships of deeply ingrained tendencies of activity in the personality. We assume that all so-called "therapies of change," which aim to alter the basic matrix of one's personality, are doomed to fail.

When people come to one of our programs with a certain "problem" they want "fixed" (that is, they want therapy), their initial work is to come to terms with their somewhat unrealistic ambition to get rid of this problem. If the identified problem is depression, they want to get rid of "it"; if they are allergic, they want a cure. If they have a tendency toward addiction (tobacco, alcohol, drugs, people), they want to have this addiction removed by some kind of psychological surgery. We recommend that they stop trying to get over the "problem," and instead sink into it and get to know it. What we call allergies are often elaborate expressions of a deep fear of intimacy. Dependencies often mask an underlying issue of faith and commitment. "Depression" is often an umbrella term for mood tones that are socially unusual yet very life extending.

In short, *there does not need to be any problem at all!* We are not diseases to be cured. We are unique human beings, each with our own history, tendencies, and ways of experiencing life. If we relinquish our ambitious (and fruitless) desire to approach the "normal," we can more readily come to grips with who we are. Instead of therapies of change, we propose an *educational uncovering* and *revelation*, wherein each individual can become more aware. The key is to stop trying to get away from oneself and settle more deeply into one's experience. Then something wondrous can occur.

TRANSFORMATION

Although it is not possible to change one's history or deep structure, one can transform the expression of the deep structure. The basic tendencies remain; how they are expressed can be modified. This transformation is quite different from transcendence, which aims to rise above oneself. In transformation, the basic deep structure is accepted, acknowledged, and studied. Ever-deepening self-knowledge arises from such an investigation of one's tendencies. In the absence of a struggle to change these patterns, one can become more and more aware of them, and even learn to anticipate them before they manifest themselves. Hence, one achieves a relative ease and freedom. The patterns are the basic plot of the play that we are living in; if we know the lines and scenes, we can more fluidly perform our part. Just like the pianist who is free to alter the expression and tones of a piece that is thoroughly practiced and known, we have the opportunity to shift the emphasis between our various patterns (the "melodies") once they are evident.

Thus, transformation does not involve change of the deep structures; rather, it means shifts in perspectives on these patterns. The deep structures themselves remain the same; yet the expression is exquisitely varied and ever new. For example, the fascination with knives that many young children have (deep structure) can be transformed into the grace and craft of the skilled surgeon. Or the interest in incision and sharp cutting objects (deep structure) could also be transformed into the keen mental attitude of the discerning academic. The careful protection of the Self from invasion by a foreign substance that typifies the allergic personality could well be used to design foolproof security systems. In short, there are creative outlets and uses for any personality pattern.

Foreground and background can shift. Take, for example, an individual who is outwardly hard and difficult to approach, and inwardly very gentle and caring. This person could, with awareness, shift the emphasis of these two basic deep structures. The result could be a warm personality with strong definition of the Self.

CONCLUSION

In our view, change of the basic personality is not possible. Often, seeking for change is a way of anesthetizing the anxiety of nonbeing that accompanies life. To accept one's deep structures and tendencies often involves accepting this anxiety. To devote oneself to knowing one's patterns and accepting the accompanying anxiety, rather than trying to eradicate them, will allow for more self-acceptance, more self-responsibility, a greater inner strength, and a heightened self-esteem.

Transformation is the ever-unfolding expression of deep knowledge of patterns of the Self. The more deeply one knows one's patterns and tendencies, the more varied, creative, and spontaneous one can be. What others claim to be "change," we identify as transformation. Nothing new has been added. A person can only become more fully alive, more aware, more creative, more in touch with one's place in relationship to others and to the universe as a whole. In short, all that we can become is more of ourselves.

To be what we are, and to become what we are capable of becoming, is the only end of life.[1]

—Robert Louis Stevenson

To Dare

To laugh is to risk appearing the fool.
To weep is to risk appearing sentimental.
To reach for another is to risk involvement.
To expose your ideas, your dreams,
 before a crowd is to risk their loss.
To love is to risk not being loved in return.
To live is to risk dying.
To believe is to risk despair.
To try is to risk failure.
But risks must be taken, because the greatest hazard
 in life is to risk nothing.
The people who risk nothing, do nothing,
 have nothing, are nothing.
They may avoid suffering and sorrow,
 but they cannot learn, feel, change,
 grow, love, live.
Chained by their attitudes,
 they are slaves;
They have forfeited their freedom.
Only a person who risks is free.

—Author unknown

Notes
1. R.L. Stevenson, in *Bartlett's Familiar Quotations,* 15th ed., edited by J. Bartlett (Boston: Little, Brown and Co., 1980), 668.

Recommended Reading
Levenson, E.A. *The Ambiguity of Change.* New York: Basic Books, 1983.
Levenson, E.A. *The Fallacy of Understanding.* New York: Basic Books, 1972.

BOUNDARIES

Currently, much attention is given to the concept of "boundaries," especially because of the discovery of the frequency of child sexual abuse in our society. This notion seems to be a useful framework for understanding the genesis of the problem, but in practice it is difficult to grasp how these ideas can be applied in everyday life.

By adopting an essentialist point of view, we can assume that each person is born with an essential "Self" that tends toward the expression of characteristics unique to that person. That Self is mostly potential. Imagine it to be like a tender amoeba-like being, surrounded by a delicate semi-permeable membrane like that surrounding the yolk of an egg. From the outside, we tend to identify that boundary as the infant's body. However, from the viewpoint of the infant the boundary is much more complicated than that; it is a *felt* experience of where the Self ends and the other begins. Sometimes, that felt experience of the Self occurs at the bodily level. The boundary is flexible and in constant motion, similar to the pseudopods of an amoeba, alternately reaching out to experience what is happening in the surrounding environment and then withdrawing closer to the center, away from the environment.

The parents' attitudes to that child are crucial to the development of the child's boundaries. Because adults tend to identify boundaries at the bodily level, the child is subtly encouraged to do the same. However, if the child's Self does not experience safety and pleasure at the contact boundary, (s)he will locate the boundary of the Self deeper within, away from the body. It is a commonly held belief that at birth, all infants are autistic, that is, they are unable to distinguish the Self from the environment; mother and child are experienced by the child as being the same. In this boundary framework, the imagined pseudopods of a newly sensing boundary have not as yet developed the ability to sort out what exists within the boundary and what outside of it. What happens at the contact boundary will determine the nature of the developing boundary. When contact is made, the infant (or for that matter, any person) will be stimulated to a state of excitement, a readiness to respond to the stimulus.

If the quality of the stimulus of the parent (or the other person, in the case of adults) is pleasing to the child, there will occur a feeling response of being safe and nurtured, with a desire to repeat that pleasant contact. In this way, the child's boundary is likely to develop in the direction of flexibility, responsiveness, sensitivity, availability, and a movement toward others that are gradually being recognized as separate from the child. However, in life's experience, the course of boundary contact does not always run smoothly. Frequently in small ways, and sometimes in gross ways, the contact is uncomfortable. It can be too little (resulting in feelings or fears of abandonment) or too much (with feelings of being overwhelmed). It can be hostile (with resulting feelings of lack of safety), demanding or indifferent (with resulting feelings of low self-esteem). When threatened, the person learns to withdraw the boundary away from contact, closer to the Self. Especially confusing are contacts that are inconsistent and filled with double and contradictory messages.

When threatened, the person has the option of either withdrawing from contact, or remaining close to contact by defending the boundary. This toughening of the boundary results in a rigidification and thickening of the organic nature of the boundary. In this way, the boundary is converted into a fortified *wall* with diminished capacities for responsiveness and contactability. The person will then feel safer, but less of a participant in life, less alive and full.

Roles are made up of those walls. They serve the function of survival, whether they be "good" (acceptable or appropriate) or "bad" (unacceptable or inappropriate) roles. They stimulate the other to give attention, be it reward or punishment. Attention is a substitute for recognition, which we believe is a necessary component of "love." Each person craves appreciation for who (s)he is, craves recognition in order to feel good about existing. More often, (s)he is given attention for acting appropriately in response to expectations, thus ensuring that the needed other will not leave. But the Authentic Self is put into storage and life becomes full of obligations, rules, and judgment-filled morality. Spontaneity, fullness of experience, and the joy of being are all diminished. The excitability of boundary contact is replaced by a constant vigilance to ensure that the expectations of others (and hence the perceived needs of the Self) are being met. The person becomes "field dependent" in a way that makes the opinions of others more important than those of the Authentic Self. Society at large identifies this process as "maturing" or "growing up," by means of which order is maintained and achievement is ensured. It is a necessary process of socialization; however, it is *not self-actualization*. Would it not be desirable to have available both of these processes, not to have them exclude each other?

Most people relate to others from their walls (that is, roles), well defended and field dependent. That seems appropriate for everyday interactions at work or in most social situations. However, it leaves people feeling isolated and unseen, motivating them to seek intimate relationships. This is frequently confused with the sexual drive and excitement, as we describe below (see "A Perspective On Sexuality"). The drive toward intimacy is a craving to be recognized, for the Authentic Self to be revealed to the other, accepted, and appreciated.

In revealing themselves, people first offer others their roles and walls. Fortunately, those are the parts that first attract others, creating a "romance," an illusion of perfection. As that romance is dying, and it usually will, the acid test of the relationship lies in the inevitable ensuing "power struggle." The choices from this point include the possibility of avoiding the struggle by separating; engaging in the power struggle by attempting to overcome the other by being "right" (or its obverse, being "wrong," as some people prefer to do); fighting to exhaustion and, ultimately, indifference or apathy; discovering ways of being creative about the struggle in order to maintain a level of excitement; or each finding ways of discovering patterns of the Self through self-responsibility and sharing these revelations with one another in order to deepen the experience of intimacy.

In an intimate relationship, each person recognizes his or her own responsibility for the Self. There is no blaming, no victim; there is only a vulnerability and a willingness to share with the other what each experiences in all encounters. The walls, defenses, and weapons are exposed to one another. In this way, each person begins to dissolve the tough hide of the walls so as to return to a more innocent and vulnerable state. Then, *real* contact is possible, and the Self can recapture the excitement of fullness at the contact boundary that it experienced in infancy. Experience is then fresh and fulfilling, albeit also frightening, sad, and sometimes disappointing.

The tragedy of child sexual abuse is that individuals frequently lose trust in their own bodies and themselves. Because pleasure is a natural function of the body, the child may have enjoyed the original acts. Sometimes that pleasure is confused by a strong wish to please the initiator of the abuse. Frequently, the sexual acts are imposed on the child, who feels helpless and unable to resist. In any event, such an inappropriate sexual act is a crossing of that person's boundary, usually by a person who him(her)self has poorly functioning boundaries. Sexually abused children will then have a mixture of feelings. They could develop feelings of guilt for having participated in the sexual abuse, no matter how helpless they were in the situation. By drawing their boundaries closer to themselves they can separate from their bodies, which they believed betrayed them, possibly because they felt pleasure in such an unacceptable situation. They could create a mythology that their Authentic Selves are unappreciated, and so they will likely refuse to reveal the Authentic Self to anybody else, being convinced that they lack worth. They tend to hide behind walls designed to project competence and self-assuredness. Actually, they live in fear and trembling that they will be discovered as frauds, acting in friendly and sometimes even seductive fashion but always in dread of sexual encounters in which they may have to perform. Any letting go is a threat to their hiding game, so they desperately try to remain in control of both themselves and others.

Once walls have been created, they serve as a prison to the Self as much as a defense against others. It becomes difficult to bring them down, to soften them back to their original function as boundaries. Too often, the wall is identified with the body, as character armour (a concept of Reich's[1]). Even if the hardened wall could be removed, as is attempted by some body therapies, that person will still have to develop some healthier means of coping with others and the environment. Experiences that heighten self-esteem and self-assertion are useful. Becoming familiar with and accepting the Self would be an even better strategy. Learning how to explore and discriminate within the environment, how to discern the intention and actions of others, is mandatory in establishing a sense of safety in relationships and in all social situations. Learning how to relate from a position of responsibility rather than victimhood is important. Ultimately, such people will develop a sense of having a right to exist as themselves, as their Authentic Selves that can choose behavior through agreement ("Yes") or denial ("No").

Although these issues about boundaries are especially graphic in the personalities of those who have been abused either sexually or physically, the principles are pertinent to everybody. Most people are working through issues related to their boundaries, afraid of being overwhelmed and made helpless with vulnerability and intimacy. Most people offer walls of self-defense, righteousness, judgmentalness, prejudices, and security instead of boundaries of contact with all their excitement, vulnerability, fear, joy, and sadness. People usually believe that in order to be accepted they must perform and succeed, impress, please, control, and manipulate others.

In order to rediscover the Self, individuals must be prepared to take risks, reveal their walls to others, and take ownership of their own feelings by being responsible for themselves. No person should define his or her self-worth through taking care of others. In every situation it is important to remember that people *do* have choices; they must take the risk of presenting who they really are and be prepared to accept the consequences of their choices. Undoubtedly, there will be hurt, but it must be realized that pain, anxiety, and sadness are as much a part of us as are pleasure, peace, and joy. To know the Self is to know these parts, all of which are worthy of sharing with one another. It is via the sharing of such aspects of ourselves that intimacy is experienced and the Self is revealed and known!

*What is asked of us in our time
is that we break open
our blocked caves
and find each other.*

*Nothing less will heal the anguished spirit,
nor release the heart to act in love.[2]*
—Raymond John Baughan

Notes
1. W. Reich, *Selected Writings* (New York: Farrar, Straus and Giroux, 1973), 53.
2. R.J. Baughan, *The Sound of Silence* (Boston: Department of Publications UUA, 1965), 7.

Recommended Reading
Perls, F. *Gestalt Therapy.* New York: Dell Publishing Co., Inc., 1951.

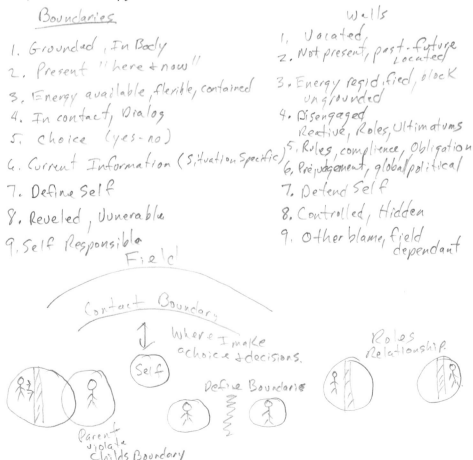

Boundaries

1. Grounded, In Body
2. Present "here + now"
3. Energy available, flexible, contained
4. In contact, Dialog
5. Choice (yes-no)
6. Current Information (Situation Specific)
7. Define Self
8. Reveled, Vunerable
9. Self Responsible

Walls

1. Vacated,
2. Not present, past-future Located
3. Energy regidified, block ungrounded
4. Disengaged Reactive, Roles, Ultimatums
5. Rules, complience, Obligation
6. Prejudgement, global/political
7. Defend Self
8. Controlled, Hidden
9. Other blame, field dependant

Field

Contact Boundary

Where I make a choice + decisions.

Self

Define Boundaries

Roles Relationship

Parent violate Childs Boundary

ACHIEVEMENT OR MASTERY

THE STRUGGLE FOR SURVIVAL

There is a commonly held belief that one of our chief tasks in life is to discover who we are. Such a theory assumes that infants are born into this world filled with the potential of becoming the persons they were meant to be. Having emerged from the womb, which provides an ideal environment of comfort and sustenance, the infant must experience quite a shock of discomfort! The safe uterine atmosphere is suddenly replaced by a hostile environment with temperature extremes, light and sound stimulation, feeding uncertainties, and a myriad of uncontrollable external factors. Threats to the infant's homeostasis (and hence its very existence) are experienced as pain or discomfort. Satisfaction of needs or the amelioration of the sources of pain are experienced as pleasure. The predictability of the satisfaction of those needs results in a comforting sense of security, which the child begins to crave while trying to avoid the experiences that produce insecurity (see below, "Strength and Power"). These basic issues of survival are primary needs that evoke a wide variety of patterns of adaptive behaviors that then become unique to that individual.

As the infant grows, early survival mechanisms are reflected in later patterns of behavior. Perhaps because of earlier (perceived) threats to survival, later issues that might be only mildly threatening to the child often provoke overreaction, with undue anxiety and tension. Children soon learn that much more pleasurable experiences ensue when they are pleasing to others. A system of mutual control between children and the people in their environment begins to be established at an early age. Children are highly field dependent, first for survival and later for significance.

Throughout life, many people are obsessed with "making something" of themselves, "being important," accomplishing something that "matters," being "significant" or "counting." Frequently, family and society encourage a view of significance that centers on achievements in the workplace and success in the establishment of a stable and loving family; a respected and economically advantageous role in life is considered to afford the highest status. However, many who have achieved these goals cannot understand their feelings of emptiness or meaninglessness, even beyond the accumulation of self-hatred that is generated by the abandonment of the Authentic

Self in striving for the Ideal Self (see below, "The Ideal Self: Striving For Perfection"). Perhaps they have confused the existential imperative to "stand forth" (and thus be "outstanding") with a societal expectation to "stand out" (and thus be "famous").

Each of us is born with our own potentials; each of us is unique. Yet we are expected to develop and conform at a rate and in the direction of the general mass of people. When we fail, we are met with exhortations (sometimes subtle, sometimes severe) to conform. Always there seems to be an expectation that we "make something" of ourselves, we become "successful," we distinguish ourselves by "standing out," being looked up to and admired. It is as though we are expected to *construct* a life of significance, rather than to *be* significant. Toward this end, doing becomes more important than being.

STANDING OUT

Because of our society's pervasive moral loathing of self-involvement (narcissism), individuals are taught to think of others before thinking of themselves; such is the readily accepted ideal of "caring." At the same time, we are expected to "stand out," to be distinctive, to be better than others but without acknowledging that this can only happen at the expense of others. This is a contradiction, a typical "double-bind" situation (as described by Bateson[1]) that for the sake of sanity, requires us to deny, repress, or rationalize it. We encourage competition without acknowledging that those who succeed do so at the expense of those who lose. They are rewarded with authority, which gives them power over the lives of others. They earn a disproportionately greater share of material wealth and are afforded a higher public status than others.

It is obvious that *standing out* provides the individual with praise and many other rewards, economically as well as psychologically. What is little understood is that such attention feeds the Ideal Self but ignores the Authentic Self; it is *not* recognition (to be "known again"). Invisible and unacknowledged, the person is left with a feeling of worthlessness and emptiness. These individuals are given accolades, but are isolated from the others to whom they are compared. In reaction, other people often experience jealousy of those who are given so much attention.

People who stand out make objects of themselves and others. Although they may have much energy to spend, they lack a sense of vitality; although they may be very active (sometimes hyperactive), they do not feel fully alive. In their striving for success they often experience tension, which they may interpret as excitement or a high-pressure charge (as can happen with big business deals). They become obsessed with accomplishments, power, fame, and the notice of others; they objectify the people in their lives, who serve to fill their craving for attention and approval. By doing so, they become markedly field dependent, their self-worth becoming tied to the amount of approval given to them by others. Because this is the usual circumstance of childrearing, it is no wonder that people commonly have a difficult time giving themselves approval and developing a healthy sense of self-esteem. Abandoning much of their Authentic Self, they concentrate on constructing an Ideal self, and in the process generate self-hatred. Their sense of pride is inflated, but their sense of self-esteem is low. They become driven to achieve more as they become trapped in a self-hating cycle (see above, "The Ideal Self: Striving For Perfection"). They are given much attention and many rewards for successfully developing and living their roles in life, and such roles often provide them with positions of power and prestige. Unfortunately, they can only feel good about themselves when they are doing and achieving.

Because the high achievers develop their sense of importance in relationship to others around them (the field), they tend to feel anxious if those others might abandon them, or merely may not be impressed. Hence, such people become obsessed with *control*. The more they can control the people and situations in their lives, the more secure they will feel and the better they will feel about themselves. This frequently becomes an issue for them at home; so long as their spouse and children are willing to be controlled by them, they feel happy. When family members take steps toward independence or autonomy, they experience this loss of control as a great threat. And so power struggles are common within the families of such people.

To stand out requires endurance, vigilance, control, effort, an obsession with details, and constant monitoring of the expectations of others. Such people are often prone to emotional instability and sentimentalism, which Oscar Wilde defined as "having the luxury of an emotion without paying for it."[2] In reacting with sentimentalism, the person disconnects from the experience itself, becoming more involved in experiencing the feeling than in remaining connected with the actual event. People who stand out become *independent* and *individualized*, remaining greatly field dependent, and continuing to rely on the attention of others for their self-esteem.

STANDING FORTH

People who stand forth become *autonomous* and *individuated*. They derive their self-esteem from their own sense of jobs well done, from their own appreciation of their having given a task their best shot, being all they can be. To them, the result is not nearly as important as the quality of the process of their doing. They feel fully behind whatever they undertake, and experience life as being full of interesting possibilities for exploration and growth. True, they are self-involved, but not at the expense of others. They remain connected to others, sensitive to the needs of others as well as to their own. They have a great capacity for empathy, while rejecting any temptation to feel sympathy (which would be condescending, arising out of an up/down situation). They recognize and respect the boundaries of others, yet are always interested in vulnerability and intimacy. They care about others while refusing to take care of them, recognizing each individual's potential for being responsible for the Self.

To stand forth requires the courage to be, creativity, awareness, presence, and focused attention, without sentimentalism (that is, overreaction, dramatization) or self-pity. Such individuals keep in touch with the essential Self while entering the world with a fullness, being as much of the Self as is possible at that time, and remaining connected with the background from which they are standing forth. Such people express the best of the human condition, evoking inspiration in others. In such a distinguished presence, people usually desire to be connected with one another, being reminded of their own potential to be fuller and more of who they are. Only when they fail to be fully who they are do they revert to resentment and blame.

Basically, the people who stand forth develop mastery of their own skills; these are not so much learned as they are revealed and exercised. To them, the pleasure is in the doing rather than just in the achieving. Because it is in them to do, their skills are a real expression of themselves, a mastery. In contrast, people who are driven to achieve often work hard at developing skills that are not an expression of themselves; they achieve competence but not mastery.

Coming into Existence Non-Existence	
↙	↘
Pain	Pleasure
Insecurity	Security
Standing forth (*coming into existence*)	Standing out (*becoming noticed*)
Self-reliance	Field dependence
Revealing the Authentic Self	Constructing the Ideal Self
Mastery	Achievement
Revelation	Strategy
Vulnerability	Control
Recognition	Attention
Strength	Power
Authentic Self	Ideal Self

People who stand forth are outstanding in the world, in the manner in which they live and create life; they fully appreciate the meaning of "coming into existence." They understand, accept, and appreciate the world of objects from which they have emerged, yet they are not controlled by it. Rather than becoming field dependent, they remain in touch with what they desire to do; they follow their hearts. Thus, they become more spontaneous, self-reliant, and self-motivated. They are more in touch with themselves and others, more fully human and fulfilled. Instead of achieving their tasks, they master them (that is, they fine-tune the skills that emerge from within rather than imposing on themselves the artificial task of acquiring some skill for which they are not suited). They increasingly reveal who they are to themselves and to others, so they enjoy much recognition (as opposed to the attention given to achievers). They experience the "oneness" of spirituality without striving for it or even naming it. As they stand forth, they recognize that they just "are," and they exist; everything just "is," and it is good.

"To venture causes anxiety,
but not to venture is to lose oneself" [3]
—S. Kierkegaard

Notes

1. G. Bateson, *Steps to an Ecology of Mind* (New York: Ballantine Books, 1972), 271-78.
2. Oscar Wilde, in Edgar A. Levenson, *The Ambiguity of Change* (New York: Basic Books, 1983), 33.
3. Søren Kierkegaard, *The Sickness Unto Death*, Walter Lowrie, trans. (Princeton, NJ: Princeton University Press, 1941), 43-44.

Recommended Reading

Tillich, P. *The Courage to Be*. New Haven: Yale University Press, 1976.

ANGER

All feelings generated within a person are based upon that person's interpretations of reality (see above, "A Model For Communication"). Nobody can make me happy or angry; I become (make myself) happy or angry over what I perceive and interpret others as doing. In this way, I alone am responsible (but not to blame) for all my feelings. When I fully understand this, I can step out of the victim role and take charge of my emotional life, developing a strength that furthers my personal growth. In that process, the power inherent in the victim role is abandoned in favor of effective communication.

Feelings are the colors, flavors, and tones that accompany experience, and they depend on related past associations and experiences. Favorable feelings, such as pleasure and joy, tend to motivate the person to reproduce those experiences. Unpleasant ones, such as fear and repulsion, serve as signals for self-preservation and tend to drive the person to avoid what causes them. If these become confused, as when a person is driven to reproduce behaviors that result in negative emotions such as pain or fear, that person will likely lose trust in the Self as well as in others.

It is our assumption that there is one primary underlying drive in human experience—the drive toward unity and joining, to return to the sense of oneness that ended at birth (let's call this "love"). The feelings of separation accompanied by a basic primordial fear of annihilation (see below, "Anxiety: Friend Or Foe?") cause us all to experience deep anxiety and feelings of aloneness. This motivates us to establish meaningful relationships in which we might re-experience that sense of union which is referred to as "love." When that is interrupted or unfulfilled, we experience frustration, fear, helplessness, or some variety of emotional pain, which motivates us to act. The infantile wish would be to control those upon whom we depend to meet our basic physical and emotional needs. Crying and the myriad of other forms of complaints are common ways of attempting to bring our caretakers under our control. If these do not readily work, we experience frustration, more fear and helplessness, and then *anger*! Anger is a final attempt to overcome the helplessness that can arise as a result of prolonged frustration. Often, the anger is directed against the person or persons who are interpreted as the source of frustration of the need. If this does not work, the anger may become directed against nameless others or against the Self.

Within society, many moral judgments proscribe anger because of its negative effects upon others. However, a closer look will reveal that the anger itself is not dangerous or destructive. What produces problems is the use of anger for control. When that happens, the anger is expressed in ways that *cross the boundaries* of others; this we refer to as *violence*. Such violence occurs even when positive feelings are expressed in ways that violate those personal boundaries, without the agreement of the recipient. Many parents "love" their children in violent ways, forcing them to do many things "for their good." When people reveal that they are afraid of anger, it is usually because in their earlier experiences anger was always accompanied by violence, usually physical but sometimes mental or emotional.

If anger can be shared in an open and responsible fashion, without blame or control, the Self stands revealed and vulnerable; this could be an opening for intimacy. In relationships, such sharing involves an engagement between the persons, an intimate contact with an accompanying sense of aliveness and excitement. However, to be able to do so requires the establishment of some fundamental guidelines:

1. There must be an agreement to absolutely no violence, that is, everybody's boundaries must be respected so that nobody will be hit or hurt in any physical way.

2. There must be no physical damage to material things other than those designated and agreed to by all parties concerned, for example, pillows that can be punched or sheets that can be torn.

3. Either person can call a stop to the proceedings at any time, especially out of fear or concern for either party.

4. The boundaries of location and time (for example, for fifteen minutes, in the living room) must be agreed upon before starting. Extensions can be negotiated at the end of that time.

5. The inclusion/exclusion of third parties (for example, the children or other members of the household) must be agreed upon beforehand.

6. The use of blame, foul language, put-downs, and so on should be allowed in the beginning, with the proviso that at the end these will be owned in a responsible way. However, these can be negotiated in specific cases, should they violate a person's baseline of acceptable behavior.

In effect, the above agreements remove the possibility of using anger to control one another through violence, thus allowing that kind of energy to be shared, to deepen the intimacy in the relationship. It is important that at the end of such sharing, time is spent in clarifying the issues that underlie the generation of anger, being careful to use the communications model (see above, "A Model For Communication"), avoiding blame and rightness. Each person must accept the responsibility for his or her own feelings in order for this to work.

From this point of view, anger is never seen as a *primary* feeling; usually, it masks a *hurt*. The cause of such hurt can be a variety of things, such as having an expectation that another person will behave in a certain way. When expectations are not met, the person with the expectations may experience disappointment and possibly much emotional pain. Instead of experiencing that pain, which would contribute to a feeling of helplessness, the person may unconsciously convert the pain into anger. Anger provides an energy that fills the person with a sense of power, overcoming the desperation of helplessness; at the same time, the anger can be used to bully or manipulate the other person into living up to the expectation. This usually works because people are so ready to accept blame and responsibility for other people's hurt. Also, because of past childhood experiences in which anger was often accompanied by violence, people are intimidated into compliance.

Some people confuse assertion with anger and violence. When people stand firmly behind their convictions about themselves (not to be confused with firm convictions about morality, a self-righteousness that sees others as being wrong), they stand forth from the crowd (see above "Achievement or Mastery"). In being with others, they assert who they are without apology and without soliciting the approval of the crowd. Because such people tend to be easily identifiable—they tend not to blend in with the crowd—they are often seen to be intimidating, angry, and rebellious (sometimes they are). It is important for such persons to know the difference; if they are rebellious, they remain tied to the crowd, perhaps becoming independent yet missing the opportunity to be autonomous. The rebel is violent, reacting against the authority of others, wanting to cross those boundaries. Self-assertive persons confirm their own being independent of the wishes of others; at the same time they remain sensitive to the rights of others, as well as their own.

If anger is not expressed directly, it finds outlets in a great variety of indirect ways. A hostile person can be smiling and friendly while manipulating events to hurt the other person. Negative gossip behind a person's back and undermining the other person's authority or credibility are common expressions of repressed anger. Sometimes anger is masked by an overniceness and overattentiveness that is an attempt to compensate for negative feelings. When anger is not expressed directly, it wears on the individual in the form of psychosomatic symptoms such as headaches, stomach ulcers, colitis, teeth grinding, hypertension, and sleep disturbances (including nightmares). In some instances the anger is directed against the Self, resulting in depression, addictions, and a wide variety of other self-destructive behaviors.

Instead of being repressed and masked, anger can be transformed and expressed in socially acceptable and self-enhancing ways. Participation in aggressive sports and competitive games are two examples of such a strategy; but even these can be destructive when the pleasure in the sport is converted into an obsessive need for dominance. Anger can also be used to ignite the aggressive drive of the crusader and political critic who serves to keep society informed about its shortcomings. It can motivate the individual to rise out of conditions of poverty and helplessness through education or advancement in employment. In all of these examples, the constructive element of such transformations is lost when the individual loses sensitivity to the rights and boundaries of others; at that time, anger reverts to being destructive and anti-growth in its effect.

Anger serves a useful purpose in mobilizing people's energy into action, lifting them out of a state of helplessness and sometimes depression, and directing individuals toward resolution of a problem. However, if anger gets tangled up with blame, treating the Self as a victim, then it becomes involved in a malignant pattern of seeking revenge. It becomes obsessive and hateful, breaking up relationships and tending to leave the person isolated and more insecure. Rather than increasing the person's vitality in life, as it can do when it is shared, such anger wears out people's bodies and feelings, rendering them less effective in life.

Recommended Reading

Bach, G.R. *The Intimate Enemy*. New York: Avon Books, 1970.
Lerner, H.G. *The Dance of Anger*. New York: Harper and Row, 1989.

ANXIETY: FRIEND OR FOE?

Western traditional medicine has viewed anxiety as a symptom of an underlying disorder, or a cause of many psychosomatic disorders, and so has devoted much attention to the eradication or suppression of anxiety. An alternative view, such as that of the existential philosophers and clinicians, sees anxiety as a basic phenomenon of life, underlying all change, growth, evolution, and sociocultural achievements. Only when it becomes severe, incapacitating or interruptive to the person's life adjustments, does it take on neurotic characteristics and hence become an appropriate subject for medical intervention. However, most people (including most physicians) have some difficulty in discriminating between ontic (existential) anxiety, which can be accompanied by many positive adjustments in a person's life, and neurotic anxiety, which can lead to many debilitating syndromes.

Frequently, because the differences between these forms of anxiety are not easily appreciated, all anxiety is treated alike. Through the indiscriminate use of tranquilizers prescribed by a physician, or the use of socially accepted chemicals such as nicotine or alcohol, the individual attempts to "cure" or alleviate the anxiety state. Lately, nonmedical drugs such as marijuana or cocaine have become more popular, used both for pleasure and for relief of anxiety. We are becoming a people of low frustration-tolerance, unwilling to experience more than a slight level of pain physically as well as emotionally. Drugs help to relieve the symptoms without attacking the underlying causes. At the same time, they contribute to a blunting of life's experiences, a levelling of the human condition to one of tranquility and mediocrity.

We have created "peace without progress," "tranquility without a sense of meaning." This dilemma is dramatically encapsulated in the play *Equus* by Peter Shaffer, in which a psychiatrist struggles with the moral implications of therapeutic intervention:

> My desire might be to make this boy an ardent husband—a caring citizen—a worshipper of abstract and unifying God. My achievement, however, is more likely to make a ghost![1]

The very state of being alive produces this chronic state of tension known as ontic or existential anxiety. Among the animal kingdom, this is a state peculiar to humans, who are capable of apprehending their own death. Rollo May said that "animals have an environment, human beings have a world."[2] The difference is that human beings have the capacity to become aware of the contexts within which they exist, along with the complex interrelationships that accompany such an appreciation. This apprehension is vast and incomprehensible, beyond reason and control—hence, the chronic state of ontic anxiety. In an attempt to cope with this anxiety, each of us develops a particular life-style. Such life-style patterning underlies the development of family, friends, culture, and the very fabric of society itself. When this life-style patterning does not adequately contend with, or incorporate, this baseline anxiety, the individual then establishes behavior patterns that give rise to more anxiety. In a cyclical fashion, such anxiety grows on itself, out of control and debilitating to the person. It is manifested in symptoms involving body, mind, and emotions; such is the pattern of neurotic anxiety.

Ontic anxiety is rarely experienced in its pure form; generally, individuals are unwilling to experience much of it, quickly defending against it or converting it into neurotic anxiety. Remnants of ontic anxiety persist in such feelings as isolation, meaninglessness, vague restlessness, discontent, and doubts about life. There is often a questioning of purpose and goals. Sometimes there is a discernible underlying feeling of despair or a sense of abandonment of the Self. Life loses its color and intensity; nothing seems worth doing. Long periods of sleep are common, unlike with neurotic anxiety, in which sleep is often interrupted (while either can be the case with depression). The person primarily loses any *reason* to live, and secondarily the *will* to live.

Humans are offered a variety of standard meanings, activities, and goals to ameliorate, mask, and cope with the *dread* of nothingness, the *meaninglessness* of life. At birth, the child's experience of the world must be confusing and anxiety provoking: how can sense be made of such chaos? From a constructivist point of view "reality" is, as we have seen, organized through the use of the following intelligences: Linguistic (language), logical-mathematical, musical, spatial, bodily-kinesthetic, and personal.[3] Through the use of these intelligences (see above, "A Model For Communication" and "Constructivism") and by utilizing information provided by parents and others, the child gradually develops a sense of the Self in relationship to the rest of the world. This sense of location, of finding one's bearings, provides a *grounding* that helps to deal with the underlying ontic anxiety. The more these intelligences are developed, the more secure the person will feel. Many people experience great anxiety when they find themselves in a foreign country, unable to make effective use of verbal communication; it is even worse when body language is misinterpreted. Extreme loss of those intelligences is considered symptomatic of mental illness; relative losses result in a state of confusion in which it is difficult to make sense of life.

In infancy, the dependent mother-child relationship is the commonest and most profound solution to ontic anxiety. This pattern is reproduced in a wide variety of ways throughout the person's life, forming the structure and meaning of all later interpersonal, social relationships. Power, control, and fame are common masks of meaning. Spirituality, morality, religion, culture, creativity, skill mastery, and personal development are some of the more acceptable solutions. Ontic anxiety underlies and motivates all of these. With the individual's courage, they flower in face of the ever-present threat of extinction.

The infant feels protected from the threat of death in the arms of the parent. Such a sense of security is essential to the existence of each person. While a child is experiencing meaningful relationships, the core feeling of isolation and dread is temporarily relieved. Thus, it is no wonder that people feel compelled to discover and maintain intimate relationships throughout life. The more that the person views such relationships as a solution to the existential problem, the more dependent, obsessive, and compulsive they will become. Such relationships are immersed in the fear of abandonment, field dependency, low self-esteem, manipulation and control of the other, power struggles, and a fixation on romance.

If and when individuals come to terms with ontic anxiety, their relationships become less dependent, characterized more by a sharing of two autonomous solitudes rather than a melding of two individuals into one. It then becomes possible for two people to become more, rather than less, of themselves in relationship! The relationship becomes more like a garden, in which each individual will thrive, attached to the other by free choice, rather than like a trap, in which each person becomes contracted, attached to the other by fear. In the free choice situation, the ontic anxiety is dealt with constructively; in the dependent relationship, the ontic anxiety is covered over and ignored. However, both are means of coping with ontic anxiety. Satisfying relationships provide a sense of intimacy that successfully deals with the ontic anxiety. Without satisfying relationships, the individual experiences a relative sense of loneliness that, in the extreme, becomes a feeling of isolation. The less the degree of intimacy, the more that control becomes necessary.

Early in development, besides having their basic needs provided for in more or less satisfactory ways, children are taught systems of behavior that are judged "good" and "bad," designed to help the individual to adjust to life in that particular society. These constitute the *moral codes* that children must learn. Conforming to those codes provides people with acceptance and value, increasing their sense of security. Amoral behavior exposes the individual to social pressures and ontic anxiety. On the other hand, antisocial behavior serves to provide a sense of meaning to the same extent as does social behavior, albeit in oppositional ways. It is easy to assume that the most anxious will seek the strongest kinds of moral solutions, either for or against. Righteous, fixed, and fundamentalistic attitudes reflect such a case.

In most societies, the moral solutions to the ontic dilemma tend to become codified into systems of religion, which provide useful and effective ways of coping with meaninglessness and emptiness. Most often, the conservative religions tend to expect strict adherence to moral codes, thus encouraging a dependency that helps to relieve the ontic anxiety. More liberal religions promote a sense of personal freedom and the development of more individual responsibility and autonomy; although this is a more anxiety-provoking path, it is ultimately a more personally liberating and growth-inducing one. Conservative approaches offer more hope and more relief from ontic anxiety, with less personal risk; so they are more appealing to people. Everyday attitudes (not only in matters of religion) of righteousness, judgmentalness, fixed opinions, prejudices, rigid morality, a strong belief in right/wrong, intolerance, and an authoritarian control over the behavior of others all reflect a *moral solution to ontic anxiety.*

Moral solutions (the codes of right behavior) are primitive manifestations of an underlying, deeper process—the *spiritual* (the sense of meaning in life). Although the drive toward the spiritual is present throughout life, it is not easily appreciated or understood; so, primitive moral solutions are readily accepted in its place. In recent decades, many people have rebelled against the control of western religions, seeking the liberating truths of eastern spirituality, only to make another religion of those spiritual paths, sometimes complete with "guru" leadership. The authentic spirituality underlying all religions can be discovered on a personal level. It does little good to exchange one religion for another when personal responsibility is abandoned. In the quest for meaningfulness, there is always a great temptation to adopt the stable hope of the moral instead of wrestling with the insecurity and questioning that can lead one to experience the *faith* that can be attained with the spiritual (we define "faith" as "the felt sense of the assurance of the continuity of life"). Spirituality must always be a personal experience; it can be shared with other people but cannot be imposed upon them. When that happens, it takes on the aspects of control, developing into a religion.

Moral solutions provide measures of control that further the aims of society. For the individual, the internal experience of ontic anxiety is replaced with an underlying feeling of guilt; in the extreme, such guilt is experienced as condemnation, and relief from guilt produces a sense of grace. Spiritual solutions, by contrast, face the absolute sense of meaninglessness and the relative experience of emptiness; the spiritual solutions provide a sense of meaning in life.

On a collective level, meanings in society are reflected in cultural pursuits such as music, art, crafts, literature, and the performing arts. On a deeper, more primitive level, people rely upon mythology to provide their sense of meaning. Each culture has its own typical expressions, although the underlying patterns are apparently similar. Productivity can take on the characteristics of a religion, often at the expense of these cultural pursuits. However, in the end, all such activities serve to deal with ontic anxiety; not all necessarily further personal growth.

Through parental guidance at first, and then through mass education, each person primarily copes with ontic anxiety through the development of *roles*. These provide a sense of purpose in life, a direction for the expression of inner energy, and a feeling of power among and over peers. Because roles are so related to the context in which they are developed, they increase the individual's field dependence. The loss, real or threatened, of these roles reveals the underlying ontic anxiety, often experienced as a sense of helplessness or depression. Such might occur when a mother loses her role as provider and caretaker as her children grow up and leave home, or when a person is fired from a long-time job, or when long-term relationships come to an end through divorce or death. The extent to which the individual in each of these cases has defined the Self in terms of these roles will determine the extent of resulting helplessness and anxiety. On the other hand, the individual who has developed a personal sense of meaning through being mindful of inner authenticity and being true to the Self, in face of the expectations of others, will be able to accept such losses with equanimity and faith.

Ontic anxiety provides the drive toward self-expression and meaning, and the spice for the enjoyment of life, so long as it remains related to the Authentic Self. When a person becomes more dependent on the approval of others, ontic anxiety is converted into neurotic anxiety, with a threatened loss of power in life. When neurotic anxiety is treated with chemical medications such as tranquilizers, there exists the danger of concomitantly dampening ontic anxiety, and hence the zest for life. This loss of zest also occurs in people who abandon their Authentic Selves to adopt their roles in life, afraid to take personal risks in their pursuit of happiness. To paraphrase a biblical saying, For what is a man profited, if he shall gain the whole world (security), and lose his own soul (meaning)?

When we walk to the edge of all the light we have and take the step into the darkness of the unknown we must believe one of two things will happen—there will be something solid for us to stand on, or we will be taught to fly.

—Claire Morris

Notes

1. P. Shaffer, *Equus* (Harmondsworth: Penguin, 1977), 107.
2. R. May, E. Angel and H. Ellenberger, eds., *Existence: A New Dimension in Psychiatry and Psychology* (New York: Basic Books, 1958), 62.
3. H. Gardner, *Frames of Mind: The Theory of Multiple Intelligences* (New York: Basic Books, 1983).

Recommended Reading

Hanson, P. *The Joy of Stress.* Agincourt: Gage, 1989.

May, R. *The Meaning of Anxiety.* New York: Pocket Books, 1977.

Tillich, P. *The Courage to Be.* New Haven: Yale University Press, 1976.

Perspectives on Guilt and Shame

The concepts of guilt and shame are commonly misunderstood and frequently confused one with the other. It is possible to be specific about the definitions of each so that they can be more readily distinguished and understood.

The psychological and philosophical literature of the western world has dealt almost exclusively with guilt, and has given very little attention to shame. The main trend in western theology and religion has also followed in this vein: guilt is seen as a common human condition, and shame is rarely mentioned. When shame is recognized, the tendency is to value it negatively: shame is a condition that one would rather not have. The popular admonition "Shame on you" speaks of our sociocultural bias against this phenomenon; when one is displeased, one wishes shame on another, like a curse. More to the point, the phrase "Shame on you" is usually used to mean "Guilt on you." Guilt is seen as a social necessity. Nietzche suggested that guilt is a payment one makes in a debtor-creditor situation; the currency of guilt holds the fabric of society together.[1] Although Nietzsche himself did not prize guilt, he recognized that the culture at large does tend to value it in a positive light. If one does something that disturbs another, one can expiate one's shortcomings by the feeling of guilt. Guilt is a currency by which one makes reparation for wrong-doings against another; much of western culture is founded upon guilt as payment.

In classical oriental culture, the situation was reversed. Guilt was considered a common human experience that is not especially desirable. On the other hand, shame was seen as a highly prized state, one that is very important and valuable. In Buddhism, shame is seen to be one of the wholesome states of consciousness, along with faith, mindfulness, scrupulousness, selflessness, and empathy.[2] Although there is a cultural heritage in the Orient that prizes shame, modern times have brought westernization to the Orient, and guilt is highly valued there as in the west. To appreciate the classical Asian perspective, one needs to comprehend attitudes from ancient times.

In studying guilt and shame, we find numerous paradoxes: although east and west had different assumptions about guilt and shame in their history, current practice elevates guilt in both cultures, and does not prize shame.

THE GARDEN OF EDEN

The philosophy of our western culture has been organized around guilt, devaluing shame. The story of the Garden of Eden provides a mythological underlay for much of our attitude. The usual interpretation of the Book of Genesis has Adam and Eve as wrong-doers. They were bad for following the advice of the snake, who represented evil. God, in his goodness, had laid down a law, which Adam and Eve broke. God exacted a punishment in banishing them from the Garden. Adam and Eve were guilty. As prototypes, they had set the tone for human experience wherein each human being must live amidst the guilt of the original sin. God is good, and a just judge who exacts retribution; Adam and Eve committed the wrong-doing in listening to the snake, who represents evil. From the moralistic viewpoint, Adam and Eve had to pay for their wrong-doing by feeling guilty.

However, there is another way to view the story. In the beginning, Adam and Eve felt, not guilt, but shame in their *recognition* of themselves. They felt guilt only later, in contending with the punishment of the wrathful God. In other words, they felt shame in reference to themselves, and guilt came later only in relation to another. In shame, they acknowledged themselves and were vulnerable. When their shame was converted into guilt, they became field dependent and objectified as wrongdoers. Their shame, which was personal, became impersonal guilt. This prime myth of our culture has cast us into field-dependent, depersonalized conditions. Each person has the challenge to wake up to shame, and move beyond the original sin (guilt) of the Garden.

DEFINITIONS

We define "guilt" as a complex of feelings involving regret, self-recrimination, depression, anxiety, and fear of punishment, arising from having transgressed some code of behavior originally defined externally. "Shame" is defined as a feeling involving embarrassment, exposure, remorse, and anxiety, arising in the recognition that one is not all that one could be. Jean-Paul Sartre put it this way:

> I am ashamed of what I am. Shame therefore realizes an
> intimate relation of myself to myself. Through shame I
> have discovered an aspect of my being . . . Shame is by
> nature recognition. I recognize I am as the Other sees
> me.[3]

Guilt arises in reference to the external, and is depersonalizing. In feeling guilt, one is defining oneself as a transgressor of some externally based code. So, guilt involves a deadening of the personal Self, oriented toward the depersonalized, objectified state. Shame, on the other hand, arises within the person in the recognition that one has fallen short of what one could be. In shame, one feels vulnerable, exposed, and very present. This condition is like what the existential writers referred to as existential guilt; shame is in reference to the Self, and is highly personal.

Thus, guilt is impersonal and shame is personal. In shame, the Self is present; in guilt, the Self is denied. Guilt is a social convenience; one feels guilty in order to get off the hook for what one has done. It has been said that guilt is just an excuse to go on doing exactly what you have been doing without awareness or desire to change; guilt then is a cop-out. Shame involves a recognition of the Self, and thus is a condition where change is possible.

MORALITY

Existential writers have proposed that humans ultimately deal with being in the face of nonbeing (the ontological or ontic condition): in being alive, we are faced with our own death as a possibility. The ontological issue is: being confronted by nonbeing; this is the absolute condition, the underlying stratum, of our human existence. Because of this, we have at the root of our existence a mammoth, all-pervasive feeling of anxiety (often called angst or dread or existential anxiety). In relative terms, this is experienced as our facing our fate. (See above, "Anxiety: Friend or Foe").

This root anxiety is basic to our existence, yet it is too awesome and huge to face minute by minute. Instead, humans convert this basic anxiety into more manageable forms—into spiritual anxiety and moral anxiety. As a spiritual concern, anxiety is felt as a profound sense of emptiness in recognizing the apparent meaninglessness of life.

Commonly, people do not want to face either nonbeing or meaninglessness, and choose to live their lives on the moral dimension of right and wrong—the realm of appropriateness. As a moral concern, the root anxiety is experienced in terms of good and bad, right and wrong. We feel anxious (guilty) when we believe we have done wrong; we feel less anxious when we believe we are in the right. This partly explains why people would generally rather be right than happy.

We learn this early. When children feel insecure or uncertain (ontic anxiety), they interpret this as a fear of abandonment. The parent figure who protects the child seems to stand between the little person and the assaults of the universe. If the parent is pleased, the child can continue to feel secure in the protection; a displeased parent could leave and the child might succumb to malevolent forces. In simple terms, the child can feel better by pleasing a parent figure. In this way, the child initiates a life-pattern of trying to live up to the expectations of someone else, and begins the pattern of field dependency. One shifts the focus from inside the Self to an external authority. If one can please one's parent, then one will not be abandoned by the parent, and hence will survive. At the root of appropriate behavior, there is a life and death issue: one wants to be acceptable in the other's eyes in order to avoid being abandoned.

As children grow, they gradually build up a picture of the parents' expectations; this is internalized ("the superego introject" in psychoanalytic terms; also called the "Ideal self"). This internal voice becomes a harsh taskmaster, an internalized authority that the individual carries around. The internal judge becomes even more demanding than the original parents. When the internal judge is displeased, it harshly criticizes, and "beats up" on the person. The judge's reprimands tell the person that (s)he is bad and needs to be punished. The form of punishment is guilt. When the person feels guilt, the taskmaster is satisfied that the slave is coming back under control. Thus, guilt functions to keep the person under control, to be directed by the internalized Ideal self. The guilty individual has been depersonalized, objectified; the personal fades, and the prisoner has to pay for misdemeanors by guilt.

Guilt is an expression of nonbeing, a denial of the Self. Even so, people often would rather feel guilt for having been wrong (moral dimension) than face up to the emptiness of meaninglessness (spiritual dimension) or encounter the nonbeing that accompanies the being in life (ontic dimension). Guilt involves submission to the power of authority, and a depersonalization. We lose touch with "the one who is" (because this includes the anxiety that one is unwilling to face) and become converted to the objectified one in the right or the wrong.

DISTINGUISHING BETWEEN GUILT AND SHAME

People often say, "I don't know how to tell the difference between guilt and shame." We believe that there is great value in being able to distinguish the two, both in the personal realm and in clinical situations.

Physiological Aspects of Guilt and Shame

The feelings of guilt and shame are mediated through the autonomic nervous system, which governs the vegetative functioning of the body. In general, guilt tends to be a closing, contracting activity. Because it is an expression of condemnation and objectification of the Self, the physiological correlate involves tightening, contraction, and dulling of feeling. Shame, on the other hand, is an opening of the Self, with an accompanying self-recognition. Being a very personal and vulnerable state, shame involves a flooding of the physical being, a flush. The simple question, "Do you feel hot or cold, tight or relaxed?" will help to distinguish between the two. With guilt comes a tightness and a coldness along with a sense of isolation or withdrawal and a sensation of weight or difficulty. In shame, the person is hot, flushed, and feels exposed. (S)he is aware of what (s)he has done, and in this self-recognition is responsible for having participated. Embarrassment is a form of shame.

Psychological Aspects of Guilt and Shame

With the objectification and self-condemnation of guilt, the Self is hidden and depersonalized. The individual is separated from the environment and is in a relative state of nonbeing. In shame, the experience is highly subjective and personal; the Self is exposed and is in a state of being. Guilt occurs on the moral plane; shame involves one's very being.

External vs. Internal Referents in Guilt and Shame

In guilt, the other is the referent; in shame, the Self is the referent. In guilt, there is judgment of the Self; in shame, there is self-recognition.

Shame and Guilt in Personal Relationships

In guilt, there is an attempt to control the other, and the vulnerable Self is not offered; in shame, the Self is vulnerable and self-responsible. Pride (and accompanying despair) occur in guilt; in shame, there is the possibility of experiencing humility and heightened self-esteem.

Theological Aspects of Shame and Guilt

In guilt, there is separation from the Self; this is the realm of sin (Latin "sine"—without). In shame, there is no sin, but rather innocence; this is the condition of union. Christopher Ricks put it this way: "A blush is a very important spiritual experience."[4]

Consequences of Guilt and Shame

In guilt one is fixated, and no growth is possible; with the self-recognition in shame, growth can occur. Guilt promotes dependence on the external; shame fosters a feeling of freedom and self-reliance. Guilt is usually followed by depression; shame brings remorse with a fullness of feeling about the Self. Guilt operates by obligation; shame operates in a self-responsible environment. Guilt invites punishment, retribution, and forgiveness from another; shame invokes repentance on the part of the Self.

CONCLUSIONS

Guilt in interpersonal relationships generally represents a control mechanism. It does not enhance closeness or union; rather, it operates to separate. It does tend to heighten the sexual charge related to dominance and power; however, it does not serve to bring intimacy. Guilt should be seen as an attempt to carry on doing what one is doing without any attempt to change. Guilt is the currency of debtor-creditor situations.

Shame arises in a condition of self-awareness, when the Self is very present. Hence, shame should be revered when it occurs. If people are to be close to one another, guilt is an expensive indulgence that must be relinquished. In an intimate relationship, shame is seen to be a rare situation, to be celebrated; when people feel shame, they are present and revealed to one another.

Notes

1. F. Nietzsche, *On the Genealogy of Morals*, translated by Walter Kaufmann and R.J. Hollingdale (New York: Vintage Books, 1969).
2. Lama Anagarika Govinda, *The Psychological Attitude of Early Buddhist Philosophy* (New York: Samuel Weiser, Inc., 1974), 121.
3. J.-P. Sartre, *Being and Nothingness*, translated by Hazel E. Barnes (New York: Washington Square Press, 1966), 302-2.
4. C.D. Schneider, *Shame, Exposure and Privacy* (Boston: Beacon Press, 1977), 109.

Recommended Reading

Freud, S. *Civilization and its Discontents*. New York: W.W. Norton and Co., 1961.

LOCATION

At birth, a child's major experience of the world is that of facing and attempting to organize chaos. In order to survive in such a world, children must learn to identify all the objects (including people) that come into the sphere of their senses: touch, sight, sound, smells, and taste. Depending on how pleasant or unpleasant these experiences prove to be, children gradually build up memories of where *in relationship to these objects* they wished to be. By doing so, children begin to make sense of their surroundings and become increasingly capable of identifying their location in relation to those objects. If they feel wanted and well cared for, they will locate the Self as a desired object in the world. When experiences are mostly negative, they will locate the Self as an undesirable and readily abandoned object in the world. This is the nature of their *primary contextual location*, which will set the emotional tone for the life-journey upon which each newborn person embarks. The primary contextual location provides the palette of affective colors (for example, sombre and serious, or bright and joyful) that an individual will use in undertaking life's tasks. These early experiences play an important part in determining which emotions a person will typically feel throughout life.

The Self with its primary contextual location faces the world and its opportunities on at least two distinct dimensions—time and space. Thus suspended in space and time, the Self of a child slowly begins to appreciate the recurrent nature of behavior; that when mother disappears from view, she will probably return (sometime in the "future"); at certain times food will appear, ideally closely following hunger pangs. Such recurrent behavior provides the basis for faith within the developing person, and trust of caregivers, especially as these experiences can be remembered in the body as well as in the mind. With growing memory, children begin to locate the Self in relation to the events along their personal time continuum. Later, they will be able to compare their location in time with that of others; but this comparison will make sense only when they are able to locate themselves in their own time continuums. Any dislocation in time will produce a sense of confusion, a time disorientation, such as what happens in sleep disorders or in behaviors that are inappropriate to the present time. People who suffer from time disorders desperately attempt to stop time, to resist change and experience less, so that their worlds will become more manageable. In the face of threatening situations, such people quickly revert to childhood, with all its helplessness and fears; usual solutions include running away, hiding, withdrawing, blaming, and becoming willful, resistant, indulgent, childishly "hysterical," or rebellious. Such behaviors become fixed in time, condemned to be repeated in a compulsive fashion, with no movement toward a real solution that could open up the world in a way that promotes healthy growth, an expanding personal space, a growing curiosity, an increasing trust in others, and a sense of faith in the continuity of life.

Life is like a voyage on a river; the passing of time is marked by events, which could be seen as docks going by our view. Because some docks are more interesting to us than others, we tend to tie our boats to those and are loath to leave them. But leave them we must, as time passes by; so we must untie ourselves from those docks (experiences) and continue our journey in time. However, if a particular experience was especially significant, whether for reasons of great pleasure or great horror, most people refuse to untie their rope from that experience; instead, they leave a long rope attached as they continue on. With their feelings, they become fixed in their location in time, although they continue their journey down the river. When faced with charged, anxiety-provoking experiences, they tend to quickly return to those docks in the past. They become limited in their ability to assess or appreciate the docks in the present. The question that they must ask themselves is, "What am I getting out of holding on to this dock so determinedly?" or "What awful thing would happen if I *did* let go of this experience?"

Certainly, most of us can readily move on the time continuum from the past to the future; but rarely are we *really* in the present. Most of us will quickly regress when faced with traumatic or risky circumstances in the present. Those fixed positions (our fixed primary locations) can usually be identified with an earlier age at which we underwent some very significant experiences, whether frightening, enjoyable, or both. From such fixed positions, we gaze along the time continuum in the direction of either the future or the past. Thus, at any given time, we have a relationship to time from some fixed time location, facing in the direction of either the past or the future.

People who resist time refuse to change their manners or morals in relation to the present. They wish to keep their lives manageable by not having to relate to things in the culture that are changing; they yearn for the familiar past. Sometimes that past contains traumatic or unpleasant experiences that continue to govern their present; for example, women who had been sexually assaulted in the past often relate to men in the present as though they *all* are going to be exploitative, thus limiting their relationships with men. Such women are handling their anxiety by narrowing their world in order to make it more manageable. To do otherwise would mean having to assess each new male acquaintance in the present. This kind of fixation on the past (frequently accompanied by a tendency to leave and/or hate the body) arose in the beginning as a means of survival; however unpleasant the results may be, it continues as a means of making the world smaller and more manageable.

More significant are the individual's experiences along the space continuum. Each person is suspended between "inner" and "outer" space. In early childhood training, people are encouraged to abandon their inner experiences to concentrate on the myriad tasks in transitional (outer) space that are essential to survival (for example, walking, talking, reading, self-care, social niceties and consideration). It is in this transitional space that one meets and learns how to control the significant others in life. Of course, we do not locate ourselves only in relationship to either ourselves (self-reliant) or others (field dependence). Rather, each of us locates ourselves somewhere along this space continuum, becoming more or less self-reliant and field dependent to varying (but usually characteristic) degrees. The main point is that each of us establishes a characteristic stance in life with regard to space and time, becoming more or less comfortable with our inner and outer worlds as well as our past and present time.

Our educational institutions tend to support a reliance upon outer experiences and other people, with a relative abandonment (and considerable suspicion) of inner space. Science has concentrated its efforts on gaining knowledge of the material world so as to control that world; little scientific attention is directed toward the exploration of inner space, which is becoming known as the "last frontier." Thus, we concentrate on all of our means of controlling our environment and the people contained therein; we learn to please, to manipulate, to dominate, to be nice, to display only socially acceptable feelings and behavior. The better we do it, the more acceptance we earn. Those who are good at it become comfortable, living much of their time in relation to (although not necessarily spending much time with) great numbers of people and in a great variety and volume of spaces.

People who are uncomfortable with large, unknown, and uncontrollable spaces react with anxiety; they feel threatened and uncomfortable. The most direct and undefended form of the inability (or the perceived inability) to handle much space occurs in the neurotic syndrome we know as agoraphobia (the fear of open spaces). Even though their reactions are usually less extreme, most people relate to such a situation with defenses that cluster around behaviors and physical symptoms (for example, the boundary illnesses such as allergies) that help to control the anxiety or the threatening environment. Of such a nature are the obsessions and compulsions of our everyday life, which organize our time and attention to such a degree that the underlying anxiety may never even be felt. When this is pushed to extreme, the person's life becomes handicapped by the necessity to perform such rituals (such as addictions to substances or people, compulsive work, repetitive self-destructive actions, or unrelenting repetitive thoughts). Ultimately, such patterns of behavior become medically diagnosable as representative of the neuroses. From the viewpoint of space, such people have made their world smaller and thus more manageable. Choices become limited, freedom is curtailed, and the mind is relieved of any need to face the root problems. Furthermore, by the mere fact of being medically sick, such persons are allowed to expect others to take over much of the responsibility for their lives. Others will make decisions for them, will usually supply endless attention, and will support the view of them as helpless victims of families, society, and friends. The result is the development of a society in which the helpless begin to dominate the activities of the majority; as so aptly described in a *Time* magazine article, we are becoming a nation of "busybodies and crybabies."[1]

If the neurotic solution still does not adequately handle the anxiety, people may remove themselves even further from others, and the threatening circumstances in the environment, by withdrawing further into their inner worlds, much smaller spaces in which they have greater control, where they are the unchallenged authorities. They become out of touch with others by becoming emotionally numb, unaffected by the exigencies of a normal life, which seem too much to bear. Because they are masters of that inner space, all is possible; they can feel either more powerful or more helpless, unrelated to the measurements of reality.

Each person orients the Self somewhere in the intersection of the continuums of space and time. Healthy, mature individuals (who are rare) would be able to freely move along both of these continuums, as appropriate to the situation. Such people could play like a six-year-old child with six-year-old children by regressing in time, to really express the energy of the six-year-old within. During play, these persons will freely move from inner space, where fantasies and emotions are abundantly available, to express them in outer space, where they can be shared with playmates. At the end of playtime, such persons will readily be able to come into the present in order to organize the toys and clean up the mess in the room (outer space) in which the fairies and dragons of inner space have played; they may even prepare for the future by storing the toys so that they are readily available when they are next needed.

A neurotic person has become fixated somewhere in the intersection of space and time, losing the freedom to move freely along these axes. Such a person has made the world smaller and thus more manageable, although much less expressive of the vastness of the Self. The present becomes contaminated by the past, and inner space may never find expression in outer space, which indeed may be seen as too dangerous to really enter; everyday behavior is dominated by obsessions and compulsions, with a tendency toward addictions. Instead of developing contactable, sensitive boundaries, such a person tends to construct isolating, thick, defensive walls behind which the Self feels safe though helpless, fixed in an earlier time, unable to deal adequately with the present. In the extreme, reality may be ignored entirely, as will happen in psychotic episodes. Although the most common pattern is to be fixated on the past and on internal space, a smaller number of people fixate on the future or on outer space; these are simply variations of the neurotic solution.

These days, it is common practice to treat the anxiety accompanying neurotic and psychotic reactions with drugs such as tranquilizers and energizers. Although these are useful in allaying the anxiety, they in themselves do not address the underlying personality problems stemming from the person's fixations in space and time. Indeed, these drugs tend to reinforce the person's sense of helplessness and encourage development of an addiction to help. The individual experiences a loss of faith in inner space, and an increasing need to trust authorities in outer (transitional) space who are basically hated and feared. It is amidst these kind of ambivalent love-hate relationships that the psychologically impaired person feels trapped in both time and space, living a life of restricted pleasure and meaning. It is no wonder that suicide is becoming an increasingly popular option.

In order to break away from crippling fixations in time and space, individuals need an understanding, supportive environment that offers more educational, felt (affective) experiences of freely travelling along the time/space axes. Along the way, people must directly address the fears that trigger the spontaneous flashbacks to past time and space. Also, they must learn how to let go of past fixations that have been used to anchor the Self in the safe port of the other, if they are to find the safe port within the Self.

Notes
1. L. Morrow, "A Nation of Finger Pointers," in *Time*, August 12, 1991, 48.

Strength and Power

Newborns enter this world with the *potential* to become responsible, fully alive human beings, to flower into a full expression of themselves. How much of the Self will develop depends on a vast variety of factors (such as family circumstances, the culture, and educational possibilities) that each person will experience, and the choices that each will make along the way. During everyone's life voyage, the *value systems* of the family and culture have a strong influence on the development of their own personal values.

Infants' first experiences of life must be contextualized in their feelings of helplessness; it is so all-pervasive that it will forever influence each person's future choices. No matter how well one does in life, the feelings of helplessness are always imminent. In response, each person develops personal attitudes and qualities to prevent the Self from sinking into helplessness. What western culture has offered has been an education in acquiring *power*, which we define as the state of having *control over* other people or things. Thus, power exists in relationship to the external world, always remaining dependent on the field. The more control that a person has, the more remote are the feelings of helplessness. Such feelings of helplessness are not abolished; they are only moved further away from conscious experience, buried deeper.

Although it is less well known and less valued, another possible solution to helplessness is to acquire *strength* (which some people refer to as "personal power") within the Self. Such strength exists mainly in reference to the Self, *not* to the external world; it involves the capacity to accept the Self with all its emerging qualities. Rather than developing methods of overcoming the opposition and threat of the outside world, "strength" persons discover the qualities that they naturally have; they accept these qualities (even in opposition to the expectations of others), and creatively design solutions to life's challenges that fit their own situations.

The following lists the possible choices that are open to the growing person. Although the qualities listed are opposing extremes, the human experience is a mixture of both.

Strength	Power
Pain	Pleasure
Insecurity	Security
Vulnerability	Control
Strength	Power
Intimacy	Isolation
Personal	Objectification
Autonomy	Field dependency
Boundaries	Walls
Discernment	Automatic reactions
Individuate	Individualize
Self-responsible	Victim, blame
Faith	Hope
Authenticity	Roles, Ideal Self
Mastery	Achievement
Situation ethics	Morality
Shades of grey	Black/white
Humility	Pride
Desires, choice	Shoulds, injunctions
Surrender	Submission
Presence	Absence
Recognition	Attention
Fulfilment	Charge
Responsibility	Obligations
Care about others	Taking care of others
Sensitivity to others	Sensitivity to being hurt
Trust self	Trust others
Inspiration	Admiration
Empathy	Sympathy, pity
Responsiveness	Reactivity
Self-compassion	Self-hatred
Acceptance	Blame
Shame	Guilt
Field aware	Field dependent

Pain vs. Pleasure

From early on, life experience is mixed with the phenomena of pain and pleasure. This duality is basic during each person's entire life. From the earliest days, one acquires a power orientation in an attempt to maximize pleasure and reduce pain: the world is a place to be controlled. If one were to accept *both* pain and pleasure, one could develop strength within the Self.

Insecurity vs. Security

The human organism lives amidst uncertainty and insecurity. Each moment involves unpredictable change. To the infant, who is so dependent upon adult figures to provide care, this uncertainty is accompanied by strong feelings of anxiety—a concern for organismic survival. This dread or existential anxiety is a given for the human being. The child learns to maximize security and minimize insecurity in early relationships with adults. This is the beginning of the path of power (see sections "The Ideal Self" and "Nemo: The Abyss Within"). The child learns to please the parent in order to gain parental attention and the assurance of continuing care. To the child, the parent is a potent figure who buffers against the assaults of the universe. If the parent is pleased, the child will be safe and secure and will have minimal pain; if the parent were to abandon the child altogether, the child would perish. Thus, the cry of the infant expresses a recognition of the uncertainty of life and the dependence upon an external parent agent for protection. This inner experience of insecurity continues into the adult's life. Although one could learn to accept the uncertainty of life, and gain strength in so doing, most usually we try to control the external world to maximize a sense of security.

Vulnerability vs. Control

Although the option exists to face all facets of experience, children are quickly taught to learn to control themselves and the environment, minimizing vulnerability. To maximize pleasure and security, they learn to control their parent figures, in order to gain the predictability of parental protection. These children adopt a pleasing attitude and mold their behavior to maintain parental protection. Of course, to control the parents, children must learn what the parents do and do not want, and then these children must edit their expressions in order to please the parents. So, children control themselves in order to control others. The prize is an increased sense of security and pleasure; the price is that children relinquish spontaneous expression, forfeiting much authentic, innate experience. Children learn to control facial expressions, emotions, and behavior, reading the parents for feedback of appropriateness. This becomes the prototype for subsequent relationships, and indeed for people's way of relating to all of life. Instead of accepting information from the external world and responding to it (that is, being vulnerable), people are prone to try to control themselves and their environment in order to gain more predictability. If one is willing to be vulnerable, personal strength can be enhanced by one's willingness to respond to life instead of resisting it.

Strength vs. Power

Control of the Self and over the other involves power. Whenever the individual is prepared to experience all facets of life, strength develops. In the power attitude, life is an adversary. In the strength mode, the individual is a willing participant in the life process; although there will be pain, uncertainty, and vulnerability, the individual grows ever stronger in the capacity to embrace these, along with joy and pleasure.

Intimacy vs. Isolation

Intimacy involves revelation and sharing, making closeness possible. If one attempts to control the other, a necessary distance and isolation results.

Being Personal vs. Objectification

When one is vulnerable and intimate, the individual person is revealed and personal. Whenever one operates at a distance in order to maintain power and control, both the Self and others are depersonalized and objectified.

Autonomy vs. Field Dependency

Individuals who control themselves and others in order to have the security of power are field dependent. In infancy, everything is done in reference to the fear of abandonment, which would result in the child's demise. Even when people grow up, the basic existential fear has not been addressed, and the field dependency—the necessity to please and control the other—continues. For these persons, life remains an adversary, and the fear is denied in the urgent quest for control of themselves and others. In this mode, persons are continually in a state of anxiety, fearing the responses of others. Just as the infant fears the rejection of the parent, the field-dependent adult fears the loss of control of the other. Emotionally, the loss of the other would open up the fear of death. The individual who is willing to face and embrace fear, pain, and insecurity has less need to respond to the vagaries of the others in the field. Hence, instead of "playing to the audience," this person is able to make individual decisions and is self-referential. The person in a position of autonomy is resilient, sensitive, and capable of compassion for Self and other.

Boundaries vs. Walls

Power-based people are willing to barter with life, using themselves as currency. They may appear to be very defined and clearly demarcated from others; however, power-based persons hide behind walls rather than living at their boundaries. Walls are brittle barriers, defenses that keep the outside away; they are based on fear of the other and insecurity about the Self. Unfortunately, walls do not only defend—they also diminish the ability to make sensitive contact with the environment and with others. Boundaries, on the other hand, accompany a sense of Self that comes with the strength orientation. Boundaries are resilient, mutable, and involve a sensitive relationship with Self and other. The Self is increasingly defined by active choices that contribute to making boundaries.

Discernment vs. Automatic Reactions

In the power orientation, the other is an object to be controlled; in the strength orientation, the other is another living being to be embraced and engaged. The power-based person does not appreciate the world of the other, who becomes objectified in a role (for example, as "wife"); the responses are automatic, dogmatic, and rigid. In strength, there is a subjective, humanizing *responsiveness*; in power, there is a dehumanizing objectifying *reaction*.

Individuate vs. Individualize

The life project of the person is to increasingly become individuated, *more of oneself*. Power-based activity is individualizing—becoming the appearance of a distinct entity in *reference to the outside world*; although the person looks very independent, he or she is tied to the external world by the requirement to be independent of it. Individuating involves the actualizing of authentic potentials, and the referent is internal. Individualizing has the external as the referent and has little to do with authentic being. Whereas the individualized person is either dependent (needs to lean) or independent (cannot lean), the individuated person can be interdependent (can freely choose to lean or not).

Self-Responsible vs. Victim, Blame

When people are responsible for themselves and all their actions they develop strength. To achieve power, one must have people (victims) to dominate and control; however, the victim is also involved in a power orientation, only with a different role than the dominator, a complementary one. Blame is involved in maintaining the victim role, whereas responsible people accept their own participation in any event.

Faith vs. Hope

Power involves a dissatisfaction with the present and a wished anticipation (hope) of a future change in a situation. Thus, there is less *presence* in power. Faith is "the felt sense of the assurance of the continuity of life"; it emanates from within the individual. With faith there is a satisfaction with past, present, and future; fears of both death and life are diminished.

Authenticity vs. Role

In power, one learns to play a role, to present an image for an effect; because the "audience" is external, there is a weakening of the sense of Self. Roles serve the Ideal self. In strength, there is a willingness to express the genuine Self; hence, there is an enhancement of authentic being.

Mastery vs. Achievement

In power, one achieves; although skills and accomplishments are piled up, there is no connection to the being of the Self. Hence, the achievements are motivated by external referents, not in harmony with the Self. In strength, there is a growing mastery and competence, which is not necessarily praised or even acknowledged by the external world. In power, the world is dominated, and one is distant from the Self and the rest of the world. In strength, one can have an increasing closeness with the Self, with an owning and flowering of one's responses and relationship with both the Self and the world. Mastery involves awareness of the Self and the external world, without investment in a particular effect; achievement and dominance involve investment in a particular effect. Mastery results in genuine skill development (that is, development that is native to the individual's capabilities), whereas achievement accomplishes arbitrary skill performance (that is, performance unrelated to the individual's potentials).

Situation Ethics vs. Morality

In power orientations, there is a notion of right and wrong, a morality. Hence, the power-based person follows a grid of rules and does not question the Self. In the strength orientation, there is constant reference to the Self and the values of oneself; hence, each situation is open to personal appraisal, in reference to one's own ethical standards. In situation ethics, there are no fixed external rules; instead, there is the challenge of continual reassessment of one's own values, and application of them in a way that benefits both the Self and others.

Shades of Grey vs. Black/White

Strength involves a more mature personality, by which the world is basically seen in terms of Self and other rather than in terms of good and bad, black and white. Hence, strength involves subtle shadings, whereas to the power orientation, things are clearly demarcated.

Humility vs. Pride

Pride involves an inflated sense of the Self, and is a condition of nonbeing. Humility involves a sensitive appreciation of the Self and of one's place in the world; the Self is seen as significant but its importance is not exaggerated. False humility is a power orientation wherein the Self is seen as lowly and insignificant; this involves a posturing, an unawareness of the uniqueness of the Self, and is a position of nonbeing.

Desires/Choice vs. Shoulds/Injunctions

To listen to one's own desires and to operate from personal choice develops strength; to obey shoulds and injunctions keeps the Self under control and maintains power.

Surrender vs. Submission

Submission is a power motif, involving giving up of the Self to some external person or thing; this is the other side of dominance, and is tied to it. In strength there is not submission, but instead surrender, *to the Self*. This is the spirit of D. H. Lawrence's passage in *Aaron's Rod*: "Give thyself, but give thyself not away."[1]

Presence vs. Absence

Presence is a function of strength; when one is involved in power, the individual is not present. With presence, people locate themselves at their contact boundaries, willing to experience all that there is to be discovered there, the dark as well as the light. Presence is accompanied by alertness, awareness, and fullness.

Recognition vs. Attention

To be recognized (Latin "re + cognoscere"—to know again) involves a personal closeness with the other; to seek attention objectifies the Self and the other and makes recognition impossible.

Fulfilment vs. Charge

With strength, one feels a peaceful sense of fulfilment that is inwardly nutritive. In power orientations, one experiences a charge that is driven and stressful.

Responsibility vs. Obligations

In strength, one acts in a responsive manner, sensitive to the requirements of the Self and its surroundings. In power, one functions on the basis of obligations, predetermined rules of conduct that do not consider the Self or the current situation.

Care about Others vs. Taking Care of Others

Taking care of others involves a role and a power orientation. Caring about others involves a consideration and concern for the other, which might not involve any action. To take care of others will weaken their initiative and maintain a tie to the caretaker; to care about others can involve letting them make their own mistakes and find their own way.

Sensitivity to Others vs. Sensitivity to Being Hurt

Sensitivity to being hurt by actions and comments of others is a very powerful position; anyone who accepts this becomes controlled by the so-called "sensitive" person. True sensitivity to others involves being responsible for one's own feelings (especially one's hurt) without blame and without attempting to control the other; one can be very aware and sensitive to others and still maintain one's own autonomy.

Trust Self vs. Trust Others

In power orientations, one puts trust (expectation and control) in others; one can then blame others when they do not do what one wants. In strength, there is no place for putting trust in someone else; instead, one trusts oneself and has faith in one's own abilities to discriminate and make choices.

Inspiration vs. Admiration

If one admires another, one is elevating the other and reducing the Self; this is a power-based perspective. When one is spurred on by awareness of another, one comes into a fuller sense of oneself, one's potential, and one's capabilities—this is being inspired.

Empathy vs. Sympathy, Pity

To feel pity or sympathy involves elevating oneself and diminishing the other; this is a power orientation. To empathize involves feeling close and identified with the other, seeing oneself mirrored in the other; both persons are equal and are responsible for themselves.

Responsiveness vs. Reactivity

In power, one reacts to situations in an impulsive, imprecise, programmed way. In strength, one responds with the fullness of the Self, in a genuine, spontaneous way.

Self-Compassion vs. Self-Hatred

Self-hatred accompanies the strain of trying to live up to an idealized image of the Self; in the thrust to achievement, one abandons the Authentic Self. In self-compassion, one draws closer to the Self and finds acceptance for all aspects of the Self, including its imperfections. Thus, self-hatred involves power; self-compassion encourages strength.

Acceptance vs. Blame

To blame keeps one in the role of a victim, where one is impotent and oppressed by life. To accept the Self and the situation permits a growing strength and a felt assurance of the Self in life.

Shame vs. Guilt

In guilt, one attempts to overpower and subdue the Self and bring it back into line; hence, one is objectified and not present. In shame, one acknowledges the Self and feels the flush of recognition of oneself; one can become present and strong.

Field Aware vs. Field Dependent

In field dependency, one's actions are governed by the reactions of the field; hence, one becomes shackled to externals and does not develop self-reference. When one is self-referential, one can remain aware of the field and take account of responses in it, without being dictated by them; this position is one of strength.

In summary, strength enhances being, awareness, compassion, growth, and life. Power, along with its obvious advantages of achievement, security, status, and control, is associated with nonbeing, unawareness, fixation, self-hatred, stagnation, and (spiritual) death.

Notes
1. D.H. Lawrence, *Aaron's Rod* (Harmondsworth: Penguin Books, 1950), 200.

Self-Esteem

Self-esteem is the measure by which one regards the Self, the value that one places upon the Self, the respect that one has for oneself. Commonly, the development of self-esteem is seen as related to the mirroring function in personality development. The simplistic idea is that the more value that children see reflected in their parents' eyes, the more they will value themselves; the more positive experiences that children have during their earlier years of development, the greater their possibility of developing high self-esteem. It is difficult to argue with that proposition; it makes sense. Yet, we have met few if any people who appear to have achieved such a comfortable state of being. More commonly, people seem to suffer from low self-esteem. Indeed, it seems that most of those who are successful (by the standards of our culture) are compensating for a low sense of self-esteem; it is *that* very sense of low self-esteem that accounts for the drive toward success. Many such people appear to be happy, or at least would not want to change their lives.

On the other hand, we also know some people who do not value themselves beyond the ordinary; as a matter of fact, they may believe that others have many more talents than themselves. They, too, appear to be happy. Their virtue seems to be a true humility, and they seem to be at peace with themselves and others.

Such people as we have described seem to refute the idea that a high sense of self-esteem is a prerequisite for happiness and success. As a matter of fact, because it is a current psychological fashion to fret about self-esteem, many people are striving stoically for the blessed state of self-esteem; some even believe that it was their right at birth to have been provided with the necessary environment (such as loving, highly regarding, mature parents). They believe that this was their entitlement, and because it did not materialize, they feel resentment over having been betrayed and cheated by their parents. Some people appear to be "stuck" with such feelings, believing that if even their parents could not love them, nobody else will. Is that the only way of explaining this phenomenon? Surely some people with even more difficult backgrounds have been able to come to some happier resolution with their families. What is the difference?

First, let us examine the development of self-evaluation. Very early in life, children confuse two very different phenomena: the pleasure of mastery and the pride of achievement. The pleasure of mastery appears to be inherent in the organism, providing a feeling of fulfilment when children take their first steps or learn to tie their own shoelaces or successfully maneuver food to their mouths. With mastery, children experience the intriguing rewards of discovery, as their world expands and they become increasingly more self-reliant and competent. Such children become more self-determining, motivated by an inherent desire to fulfil their potential, to actualize that which yearns to be realized, to express an inner drive to grow. In these circumstances, the best thing that a parent or teacher can do is to provide a safe learning environment and some encouraging support for such mastery to blossom.

Unfortunately, with a strong urge to be ideal parents for their ideal children, most people are determined to help their children achieve these important steps toward self-reliance through encouragement, bribery, blackmail, threats of abandonment, and any number of other coercive means. It is all done "for the child's good." Under the watchful eyes of such authority figures, children begin to recognize that what they do is always subject to evaluation, to judgments of good or bad, appropriate or inappropriate, satisfactory or unsatisfactory; furthermore, their behavior seems able to produce pleasure and displeasure in others. Such circumstances foster a field dependence wherein the evaluation of others becomes more important than the child's own pleasure of mastery; the one increases as the other decreases.

Through introjection, the child swallows whole the evaluating functions of the parents (the "superego," "parent within," "Ideal Self," and so on), and self-esteem becomes linked with this inner judging authority. The nature of this authority (harsh, easy, inconsistent, rigid) is closely related to the kind of mirroring that the child experienced. Distortions in the mirroring function (such as over- or under-estimating) can have a radical effect on the child's self-esteem. If children are underestimated by their parents, they will tend to introject an underestimating inner judge, resulting in feelings of inadequacy, unworthiness, self-doubt, and uncertainty. The natural feelings of pleasure over mastery are abandoned in favor of such an evaluating process.

Overevaluation by the authority figure rarely produces a happier situation. Such distorted (convex) mirroring may indeed produce within the child an overly great superficial sense of high self-esteem; but if it does not match an inner sense of mastery, the child intuits it to be false. In such situations, the child can develop contempt for the external authority (and then, by association, for all authority), frequently ending with self-loathing for having duped those important authority figures. Thus, although such circumstances may appear to result in high self-esteem, they are accompanied by a deeper, more dangerous self-loathing and contempt for others.

Underevaluating (concave) mirroring from a parental figure tends to produce within the child feelings of worthlessness, incompetence, and inadequacy. The child tends to incorporate this mirroring by developing an internal attitude that is critical and unaccepting toward the Self. These children grow to become self-effacing, self-doubting, uncertain adults who may be perfectionistic but are never satisfied with themselves.

Uncaring unconcern, or the parent's inability to mirror at all, will induce a child to feel invisible, unworthy, and unlovable. It is as though the mirroring process provides a stimulus for an inner tropism toward being; it may be an important factor in experiencing existence itself. Without mirroring, the psychological sense of presence that precedes self-esteem may atrophy, thus dooming to failure any subsequent attempts at increasing self-esteem; such attempts may appear to be successful, but with a lack of true ground, the self-esteem generated will be false and unhealthy. Frequently, such persons become society's leaders and role models, whom the masses look up to and wish to emulate—people like political leaders, movie idols, and rock stars. One may wonder why the average person has such a penchant for ideal role models, sometimes even being prepared to abandon themselves in favor of some ultimate authority. The search for such authorities has produced a big business in the psychological, spiritual, and religious fields.

It is often suggested that the search for ultimate authority has its roots in the craving for father, a result of inadequate fathering or some unresolved infantile fixation on the father. We believe that such a yearning *precedes* the father-child experience. It is an algorithm established at the juncture between mastery and achievement, when achievement takes precedence over mastery. In this commonly experienced scenario, the Self loses pleasure over its own mastery, instead seeking comfort and security through relationships with outside authorities that need to be pleased in order to achieve acceptance. Parental figures are the first such authorities; in a patriarchal society such as North America, the father becomes the ultimate authority, slipping readily into this previously established algorithm.

The crown of ultimate authority rests uneasily on father's head (or that of any leader, role model, or star). Because such a position is usually lacking in the pleasure of mastery (fulfilment, true self-esteem), any achievement produces more self-doubt, contempt, self-loathing, and pride (false self-esteem). Power needs become of paramount importance, control over others a goal (albeit subconscious or denied). This unfortunate scenario is reproduced at many levels of society, resulting in the unhappy circumstances of many people basking in the glory and acceptance of father-figures (of both genders), with their (surface) self-esteems apparently intact but their self-loathing growing (leaders as well as followers). History has revealed how often this scenario has been doomed to failure, ending with masses of people feeling betrayed and disillusioned. Recovery from these situations offers an opportunity to return to the important junction point of mastery and achievement, to learn from the experience, and to proceed further along the path of self-actualization, beyond achievement. Most people waste this opportunity, continuing to seek other ultimate authorities; their true self-esteem suffers.

In the current psychological climate, self-esteem has become a central goal for many therapists and educators. By making it an achievement that must be reached, they have made self-esteem the new ideal. Such striving will tend to reproduce the original problem of the self-hatred cycle. People may attain a superficial sense of high self-esteem, only to discover more self-loathing and self-hatred. We would do well to devote more attention to developing self-compassion, self-acceptance, and self-love, all as a means of experiencing a fuller sense of love with others. After all (to paraphrase the gospel of Matthew), "For what is a man profited, if he shall gain self-esteem, and lose his own soul?"

Entitlement

Entitlement is a natural occurrence in child development, in which infants believe that the world around them must provide for their wants or needs. The normal maturation process involves a gradual relinquishing of this position. Although entitlement is important at the beginning, it becomes counterproductive at later stages of development. The early phase helps to establish a sense of self-importance in relation to the rest of the world. Later, it is this same narcissistic position that stands in the way of a genuine dialogue with another. We see many people who are fixated in their entitlement phase; such fixation seems to be a phenomenon of this age.

NORMAL CHILD DEVELOPMENT

In the womb, children experience a fusion with their mothers and cannot distinguish themselves as separate. At birth, babies become physically separated; however, psychologically, for some time children continue to behave as if their mothers and the rest of the environment were part of them. As perceptual functions develop, infants begin to make out vague outlines, and slowly come to identify one of these shapes as their mother. In the same manner, they learn to make out other people and objects. At the beginning, children treat all of these objects as extensions of themselves, not separate. The project of psychological maturation involves a distinguishing of external objects and people, and an assigning of names to them. The development of language symbols provides a matrix for children to relate to the external world and build a relationship with it. Children gradually come to recognize that their mothers are separate from themselves, but they still experience a sense of possessiveness; when they are hungry, their mothers are their servants, providing for their wants; when they are cold or wet, the people who are their possessions should cater to them. This is the experience of entitlement, which is a normal phase of early child development. Between one and two years of age, babies begin to move away from their parents physically, exploring the world around, constantly checking back to see that the parents are still pleased and under the child's control. As children move forward into the world, they carry a feeling of entitlement. Just as they see their mothers as possessions, subject to their every whim and command, children apply this entitlement to the rest of the world, expecting attention and service.

In "good-enough parenting,"[1] children will encounter boundaries within their parents, whereby every little whim is not indulged. Thus, they can develop an awareness that the parents are separate and distinct entities, with personal thoughts, feelings, and desires. Children will at first try to rebel against this awareness, attempting to bring parents under their control. If parents are successful in maintaining their own sense of boundaries, their children can continue to mature toward more distinct individuated selves. In the milieu of parental boundary-setting, done in an atmosphere of caring and consistency, children can begin to move from the narcissistic, self-involved world to acquire the capacity to recognize the personhood of another, and can begin to develop a more consistent and fulfilled sense of themselves. This long journey of acknowledging and respecting others' boundaries, and learning to define oneself in relation to others, is called the separation-individuation project.

PERSISTENT ENTITLEMENT: THE ARRESTED CHILD

If children are successful in bullying their parents (that is, if parents fail to assert their own individuality and boundaries), they will not learn the valuable lessons that permit the next phase of psychological development. In order to mature beyond the self-involved infant state, children need to come up against the boundaries of their parents and discover that there is someone separate and distinct from themselves, worthy of respect and acknowledgement. Each time children do not automatically get their own way, they are stimulated to recognize that their parents are separate individuals. Indulged children, who do not encounter parental boundaries, fail to develop a concept of the separate other; as a result, these children maintain their entitled position where they are the center of the universe. Psychological development arrests, and these individuals remain fixated as entitled ones.

Often, parents themselves feel entitled to have their children be what they want (the *idealized version* of the child). Parents who have lived in the entitled state have not learned to recognize genuine otherness in a relationship; instead, such people's relationships are based on self-serving expectations, with little patience for the desires or differences of the other. Such entitled parents fail to recognize the personhood of their children; instead, they reward their children with approval and attention and encourage the development of their children's Ideal Selves. Youngsters who learn to seek approval believe that they are entitled to attention and reward when they meet the other's expectations; they are disturbed when such rewards are not forthcoming. Parents can only stimulate development in their children to the degree that they have themselves developed; the task of parenting includes with it an urgent clarion call to "grow up" oneself! If parents did not feel entitled to the idealized versions of their children, and instead were interested in recognizing the personhood of their babies, they could become a stimulus for the youngsters to grow with a separate sense of themselves, for in recognizing the infant, the parent provides a stimulus to interact in dialogue, valuing both the Self and the other.

Entitled children grow up believing that the world owes them whatever they wish. When desires are not met, they become victims of the world. They do not develop autonomous initiative, and are dependent upon the movements of others. As well, they do not develop sensitivity to others, which would permit the more advanced experience of object constancy, and a later subject constancy.[2] With this entitlement, these persons do not become individuated; rather, they remain arrested tyrants, expecting the world to cater to every whim instead of using their own initiative, will, and imagination. Hence, entitled people are stunted, weakened, and power oriented; field dependent, they are tossed about by the reactions of those they try to rule. They rage or sulk, without any capacity to learn that they will not automatically have whatever they want; thus, learning is blocked, initiative is blunted, and the loving compassion of the mature individual does not germinate. Entitled children grow up to be entitled adults, who perpetuate the cycle. There is much "for me," and less sense of the other; hence, such individuals are lonely and have a decreased capacity for relatedness and intimacy. Such people's self-regard is maldeveloped, and their personal sense of strength is retarded. Desperately trying to manipulate the world, entitled people remain tied to the others they try to dominate. To exert control, the Ideal self grows in power, trying to please; with this desperation comes a deep self-hatred and lack of confidence (see above, "The Ideal Self: Striving for Perfection").

The phenomenon of entitlement, which is a normal developmental phase, becomes an insidious malignancy when it persists beyond early childhood. Although it is possible to develop increasing sensitivity to others, and to enter into a stimulating dialogue, the entitled person remains insensitive. This individual is prone to a life of controlling others, adopting an attitude of power and domination. One of the most treacherous aspects is that self-centeredness interferes with development of self-initiating functions. Self-centeredness is rooted in anxiety about survival; entitled persons are insecure unless they are being attended by servants. Given this profound fear, self-centered people develop their view that the rest of the world is to take care of them. The result is stunted personalities, insensitive to the needs and experiences of others; such people become autocrats who are out of touch with the lives of those around. Entitled people miss those very people in the field who could be stimuli for personal development, if they were recognized.

THE PROFILE OF THE ENTITLED PERSON

The adult entitled individual, retarded in personal development, remains like a young child, irresponsible and without initiative. The attitude of entitlement is "Take care of me." The entitled person remains as a victim, feeling hurt and unhappy in this situation of field dependence. There is a lack of curiosity and much feeling of dependency upon the other in relationships. These individuals are not curious, and thus learn only what serves to facilitate the acquisition of their "due." Entitled people do not learn well from experience and do not develop a genuine interest or curiosity in the other. Hence, existentially, entitled people are trapped by expectations of what the mirages of the world will offer them. In day-to-day interactions, entitled people show little regard for others. They will stand in a door, oblivious that others might want to go through. Such persons will throw a cigarette butt onto the ground with no qualms that someone else will have to pick it up; in their minds, the rest of the world are servants to indulge their carelessness. In relationships, these people feel misunderstood when someone does not agree with them; for them, it is inconceivable that anyone else could have a valid point of view. At a table, they will take the biggest and the best items of food and will not be concerned with taking only their share. There often is a lack of forethought, with emergency last-minute plans that inconvenience co-workers and friends. In general, there is a lack of consideration for others and a belief that the world should take care of things for them. When things do not work out, they react with blame rather than self-investigation. Hence, personal responsibility is replaced by resentment of the world for not providing.

With entitlement comes a failure to develop courage. The entitled person operates from power and control rather than from the vulnerability and self-revelation that induces strength. Such people live in an objectified world and do not develop a sense of themselves or others. They individualize rather than individuate. Outwardly confident, they often lack simple social skills and live with a chronic deep-seated fear over their own survival. Unable to develop boundaries, they instead construct walls that interfere with genuine dialogue; along with walls come the "boundary illnesses" (asthma, allergies, phobias, and cancer). The control-oriented, entitled person is field dependent and does not develop the self-reliance and initiative that mark the resilient personality of someone who has relinquished entitlement. Entitled people are more prone to dependencies of all sorts (on institutions; on anesthetics such as TV, drugs, or alcohol; and on others who will support the illusion of their importance). Often, work is for security and financial gain rather than for the sense of satisfaction that comes in collaborating with other humans in a sensitive dialogue of activity and love. There is a profound lack of rest and settling, because entitled people have a poor sense of their location in the whole scheme of things. With their inflated sense of self-importance, they are out of touch with their place. There is much goal-oriented striving after the images of the Ideal Self, and less of being in touch with the Authentic Self; hence, there is more self-hatred and more self-denial. Deep down, entitled people have a profound fear of intimacy; because they do not recognize the other, they are suspicious and have paranoid fears of what others can do to them. Because they use walls rather than boundaries, they tend to be rigid, seeking clearly defined roles and expectations; thus, they are prone to a herd mentality and are stifled in their creativity.

ENTITLEMENT: A SOCIAL DISEASE OF THIS ERA

In recent years, there has been increasing evidence of entitlement as a phenomenon in society. In the sixties, a questioning of social values and a search for Self gave rise to the "I am me" generation; the current one is a "give me" generation. It appears that the increased freedom of the sixties and seventies brought more fear on the part of the individual: people seem to have recoiled from freedom and closed up in their anxiety. With rapid technological development, society has been providing for the individual; in this era of easy access to goods, people have come to expect to be provided for. What was a privilege in the fifties has become a right in the nineties. With this entitlement, there is less cooperation, less consideration of others, more "me" and less "us." Such an attitude explains stopping one's car in the middle of a busy street to chat with a pedestrian, and the pollution that comes from thoughtlessly disposing of waste products (on the individual and national levels). The spiritual values that could arise from genuine dialogue with others do not develop. Hence, in this era there is more materialism (as a substitute for spiritual values, and to provide a security that is lacking in an isolated world). So, too, in such an isolated environment there is more fear, less security, less risk taking, and less creativity.

There is less personal felt meaning and more sociocultural obligation. There is a return to conservative, authoritarian religion, with more morality and less situational ethics. We have people who are patterning themselves on cultural expectations; the result is less individual imagination and personal ethics. As a society, we have moved away from being autonomous, individuated, curious, and responsive persons; instead we have become a group of dependent, individualizing, obligation-bound, self-righteous followers. More than ever before, potent forces threaten to restrict personal development and individuation.

INDIVIDUATION

Individuals who gradually relinquish entitlement become more responsible and feel more sense of themselves, as they are initiating rather than looking for others to begin things. This attitude is crucial in moving into more mature relationships: the less entitled people are, the more they can pull their weight in a relationship. As entitlement is relinquished, more advanced psychological functions begin to sprout: imagination, initiative, personal responsibility, and integrity are born from the self-reliant, unentitled position. With respect to relationships, the more that entitlement is relinquished, the more personal the individual can become. In a dialogue, such a person will be interested in learning about the other; there will be a genuine curiosity about the Self and the other, permitting a relationship that opens up a panoramic sweep of growth, embracing life and all its challenges. Such a person is capable of true intimacy, and the self-fulfilment of a thorough engagement with life.

CONCLUSION

As entitlement diminishes, the individual can grow and develop, and stand forth in the face of the tremendous challenges the world presents. Although aloneness will increase, the sense of personal strength and self-regard will also increase, and there will be a sense of fulfilment in feeling self-compassion and self-acceptance; such persons can move into a harmonious relationship with the rest of the world, knowing their location within it. And most significantly for the person who has diminished the sense of entitlement, there is the possibility of relating with a genuine sense of the other. *Intimacy grows as entitlement diminishes.*

I have taken forty years to make my psychology simple. I might make it still more simple. I might say "all neurosis is vanity"—but this also might not be understood.[3]

—Alfred Adler

Notes
1. H. Guntrip, *Psychoanalytic Theory, Therapy and The Self* (New York: Basic Books, 1973), 113.
2. S. Cashdan, *Object Relations Therapy* (New York: W.W. Norton and Co., 1988), 44.
3. A. Adler, in Ira Progoff, *The Death and Rebirth of Psychology* (New York: McGraw-Hill, 1956), 81.

TRANSFERENCE

Especially at birth and during the earliest years, each individual feels extremely vulnerable to the vicissitudes of life, requiring food, warmth, liquids, and physical stimulation. Many have speculated that at some level, children feel a sense of terror at the possibility of being abandoned to face the elements alone. Living in dread over this possibility, children are totally dependent on the people in the environment (field dependence), and the parents are seen to be powerful and extremely important. In the early years, the parents are seen to be the arbiters of the child's fate. They are thus thought to be powerful and god-like, much bigger and wiser than the child, who in comparison feels small and helpless. For survival, infants must do everything possible to please or control the guardians of their existence.

As object relations theorists have proposed, each person needs to separate from the parents. Such separation can be done in a variety of ways. The most common way is through denying one's dependence upon parents, in order to become self-reliant and independent (individualization); this often involves rebellion and willfulness. Or the separation may proceed along a path of individuation, in which the dependency needs can be acknowledged, not denied, but also are not seen to be the chief determining factors in the person's behavior. In individuation, separation occurs more organically as individuals develop mastery of their own capabilities; the desire to separate is determined from within the person, not from outside. Ultimately, people need to decide to wear a raincoat in the rain even though their mothers told them to do so!

As children grow in competence, developing increasing self-reliance, they become less dependent on their parents for survival. However, the early fears of abandonment do not die easily. Most people, even those who are seen as the most competent in our society, still carry within them much of their early dread of being left alone, and fear that they will be unable to survive without (parental) support. This dynamic between the small, helpless Self and the wiser, more powerful other shapes much of the person's psychological development and determines the nature and quality of all future relationships.

As children grow and come into contact with people other than their parents, they assume that the new people have power and wisdom similar to their parents, because they exist outside of the Self, along with the parents.

In other words, the child *projects* onto these other people the same qualities and capabilities that s(he) has experienced with the parent. This process of transference is the child's attempt to keep the environment outside of the Self stable, controllable, and above all safe. Through this process of transference, young people create the psychological and emotional environment in which they will live and develop. If a person's earliest years were filled with experiences of rejecting and hostile parents, that person would tend to expect that these experiences will be met with in all future authority figures, as well as future intimate partners to the extent that they are seen as being parental. If the early parent-child transactions were primarily loving, that would be the character of the expectation placed upon future relationships.

In interpersonal relationships, this propensity toward transference projection ("ghosting" or "placing hats" upon the other person) makes it difficult to ever get to know others for who they really are; they are always seen through the screen of transference. Generally, it is this very screen that attracts or repels people in relation to one another. It motivates us in our selection of partners and friends: we choose those upon whom we can most easily transfer our desires and needs. These attractions and repulsions determine the nature and quality of our interpersonal relationships.

Therapeutic relationships are only special kinds of interpersonal relationships, in which the activity is directed toward helping the client. The nature of that help depends upon the therapist's orientation; it ranges from attempting to "cure" to attempting to "educate." Whatever the goal, use is nearly always made of the client's natural tendency toward transference. For some therapists, that transference is used to control the client's behavior, as a parent would a child's behavior. Others object to using transference in that way, seeing it as a means of fostering dependency upon the therapist and therapy. In any relationship, it is important to understand how the transference will be used.

It is also important to recognize that transference is invariably a two-way street. Depending upon their own needs and personality, persons in any relationship (whether personal, business, religious, therapeutic, or other) will transfer their feelings upon one another. In therapeutic relationships, the therapist's propensity to do so is referred to as "countertransference." The client's transference can be complicated by the therapist's countertransference, if it is not clearly understood. If therapists have an inner need to be needed, they will tend to cultivate their clients' dependency and interfere with their process of individuation (which process is not always a goal of therapy).

Transference can be used to foster either individualization or individuation in any kind of relationship. Individuated persons will ultimately have little need of transference, because they will be more self-determining, less fearful of being alone, and more confident in their own competence. Through recognition and acknowledgment of the transference, both parties involved will have the information they need to choose their feelings and behavior. Instead of being driven by unconscious forces, individuals can take charge of their own lives.

In any encounter between people, the transference phenomenon should be elucidated. If it is not recognized and acknowledged, each of the persons involved usually becomes stuck in a way that reflects past experiences (for example, defensive, rebellious, compliant, regressive) rather than making new and healthier individuated choices. When transference moves toward resolution, it usually proceeds in the following, somewhat predictable, stages.

The Stages of Transference and Countertransference

The magic stage is related to the "bonding stage" of the object relations developmental continuum. During this period, there is an expectation of cure. Therapists (or teachers, or lovers) are seen to be all-knowing and wise, people who will be able and willing to provide their clients with the kind of care the latter either believed they had or dreamed of having as a child.

The leaning stage is related to the mirroring stage in development, when parents reflect back to their children the latter's revealed feelings, along with parental reactions to those feelings as well as actions. In therapy this is a period of reflective interpretation, with the therapist attempting to see through the armor or facade of the Self in order to reflect the true Self. In Horney's perspective (of Ideal, Real, and Authentic Selves), the process of creating self-hatred is uncovered.[1] In psychoanalytic terms, the parental projections are explored. In humanistic psychological terms, therapists reveal their countertransference and personal reactions in order to establish a more realistic interpersonal relationship in the present; healthy narcissism and self-compassion are reinforced, and recognition of the transference process and responsibility for the Self is encouraged.

The self-reliant stage is related to the "rapprochement stage" of development, when the child is prepared to accept a separation from the parents, recognizing and accepting in them their differences, their good qualities as well as their faults. In therapy, it is a time of realistic assessment and acceptance of the differences between the client and the therapist. Each can recognize the other as a separate person capable of being intimate without losing the boundaries of the Self.

Negative transference can occur in any of the above stages. In this process, clients are unable to integrate the good and bad parts of themselves or their therapist, often believing that their therapist is not meeting their *perceived* needs, much as they may have felt with their own parents. The therapist is polarized into being all-good or all-bad; the client may terminate therapy with unresolved feelings. Hopefully, the therapist will have the opportunity to help the client recognize this process and thus achieve some useful insight into what is often a characteristic manipulative behavior.

Janet Malcolm, writing about psychoanalysis, has maintained that Freud's most original and radical discovery was how we all invent each other according to early blueprints.[2] Transference suggests that personal relations, the most precious and inviolate of entities, are actually messy jangles of misapprehensions, at best an uneasy truce between powerful solitary fantasy systems. Even (or especially) romantic love is seen to be a fundamentally solitary experience, profoundly impersonal. The concept of transference at once destroys faith in personal relations and explains why they are tragic; we cannot know each other. We must grope for each other through a dense thicket of absent others. We cannot see each other plainly. A horrible kind of predestination hovers over each new attachment we form.

" 'Only connect,' E.M. Forster proposed. 'Only we can't,' the psychoanalyst knows."[3]

Notes
1. K. Horney, *Neurosis and Human Growth* (New York: W.W. Norton and Co., 1950).
2. J. Malcolm, *Psychoanalysis: The Impossible Profession* (New York: Vintage Books, 1982), 6.
3. Ibid, p. 6.

Recommended Reading
Rosenberg, J.L., Rand, M.L., and Asay, D. *Body, Self & Soul: Sustaining Integration.* Atlanta: Humanics, Ltd., 1985.

Nemo: The Abyss Within

Most people seem to be trapped between the desire to let go and the fear of letting go. Being able to let go would offer welcome relief from tension and worry, an experience of pleasure or even ecstasy. If so, why are people so commonly frightened by the possibility? Frequently, they express a fear of "coming apart," of "losing the Self," or of "falling into a pit." We believe this to be a symptom of people's relationship to the abyss within, what novelist John Fowles called the "Nemo."[1]

From conception to birth, the foetus develops in a nearly perfect uterine environment. Some have speculated that during this time there is no separate Self; everything experienced *is* the child's self (note: not as yet the Self). In the first few years of life, the child's main project is to separate the self from the other. Initially, mother is experienced as an extension of the self, an essential part that provides sustenance and comfort. Very soon, it must become evident that in this sublime period of primary narcissism in which everything is "me," some parts of "me" begin to act beyond my control, disturbing my inner sense of peace. The breast, the bottle, mother appear to have a will of their own, coming and going at times unrelated to my wishes. Reluctantly, these uncontrollable parts of myself are deemed to be not the self, and are walled off from the self to become the other. At this point, the self is still very narcissistic, existing in all of the space up to the wall, beyond which is the other—the objects (mother, father, siblings, pets) that move in the child's space. They are desirable for the comfort, pleasure, and security that they are able to offer; they are dangerous because they appear to have wills of their own. For both reasons, they need to be controlled and subjugated to the child's will.

As children grow, the objects in their space seem to become more uncontrollable. Furthermore, there appears to be an increasing number of them occurring on the periphery of space, coalescing into an ever-growing outer space, separated now by a wall. Defensively, the child contracts the self away from those objects, thus creating a vast, empty space between. That space created by contraction becomes the void—transitional space, the abyss, the Nemo. At this point, there exists the self (still not the Self) that is defined by the wall, the void (Nemo), and the other (the first objects in the child's space). Because objects move uncontrollably in this void, the Nemo is greatly feared. Because parental figures appear to have mastered movement in this void, they are highly regarded and imbued with great power; the friendlier they are to the child, the more dependable an ally they will be, and the more relaxed the child can be. Uncontrollable objects are feared and designated as being "wild." When animals such as pets prove to be controllable, they become strong allies. Inanimate objects such as teddy bears, which resemble the wild but are completely controllable, are the most comforting allies. These kind of transitional objects help us to handle the terror of the void.[2]

Magic occurs in the Nemo; it is the locus of creativity and imagination. However, to the child, therein dwell the forces of darkness as well as the forces of light and creativity. Out of the Nemo (which is frequently located under the bed or in a closet) rise the uncontrollable monsters of childhood. But it is also the abode of fairies and angels, elves and trolls. Anything that comes from there or moves freely in it (such as sorcerers and wizards, parents and priests) is imbued with great power. It is the stuff of fascination and folklore, the sacred and the profane. In some cultures, wild animals that can negotiate the Nemo are worshipped (such as the snake, bear, and tiger) in order to control their power, or more accurately, to appease them so that they will not use their power against society.

Very early in our lives, we become involved in rituals that help us to manage the terror of the Nemo. Before the Nemo becomes an issue for us, our own bodily excretions are seen as a part of ourselves. We are then as curious about our feces as we are about our fingers or toes. But once the walls of the Nemo have been defined, we become nervous about losing our bodily wastes into the Nemo. When they leave our defined walls, they pass beyond our control, entering into the Nemo and becoming separate objects, changing our previously held confidence in the self; our human wastes are then treated with repulsion and anxiety.

At approximately two years of age, the Self is conceived; by three years of age, a Self is finally born.[3] During that important year of life, the child completes the separation of the self from the other. During the first year of life, the self is separating from the other through the construction of walls and the experiencing of the Nemo. At two years, the child is contracting behind the walls through the development of a boundary that defines the (True or Authentic) Self from within. In contrast, the walls have defined the (False) self from without, in reaction to the others. The boundary of the Self is hypothesized to be inherent to each person, a function of biology and growth. However, parenting tends to encourage the construction of a wall, the development of a False self. When the boundary is not exercised through the making of choices, the assertion of the Self, and the acceptance of responsibility for the Self, it tends to wither. Frequently, the Self is abandoned very early in life; fortunately, it is never too late to reclaim it, as so many people attempt to do later in their lives.

The task of dealing with the "real" world is primarily relegated to the False self, which has been shaped by the person's interactions with authority figures at home and in society. Control, manipulation, and the use of strategies are all defensive tools of the False self, developed at the wall for the purpose of *perceived* survival. The need for approval and the fear of disapproval are issues of this False self, creating an ever-growing field dependence. While the True Self is growing behind this wall, it faces much self-doubt as it observes the extent to which others value the False self. To the extent that the Self believes in the wall of the False self and invests emotional energy in it, there develops an increasing amount of *hubris* (the insolence or arrogance caused by inordinate pride; exaggerated self-confidence). When confronted with honest feedback from others that is difficult to hear, most people's hubris will cause them to defend the False self with a variety of mechanisms, such as rationalization, denial, obfuscation, distraction, and deflection. It is an interesting phenomenon that most people, when given the chance to reveal the True Self, will come to the defense of the False self, unless they have been able to come to terms with their hubris. Originally, that defensiveness was a product of the need for acceptance and survival; later in life, that defensiveness serves only hubris.

The Nemo is primarily the product of the building of walls. Others exist on the other side of this gap (see below, "Bridging The Gap"), creating the need for control, objectification (see below, "Objectification"), dependence, defensiveness, blame, and victimhood. The False self can be diminished through the dismantling of the wall, and the boundary of the True self can be exercised through the discovery of options and the assertion of choices. Only when these issues are addressed will the True self grow into its maximum potential.

Notes

1. J. Fowles, *The Aristos* (London, Pan Books, 1968), 51.
2. M. Berman, *Coming to Our Senses* (New York: Bantam Books, 1990).
3. Ibid, p. 34.

Bridging The Gap

Beyond the Self is nothing but a void, a transitional space within which each of us must create our own personal world. All that we perceive through our senses are objects, which we imbue with meaning. The infant will notice that some are mobile and others are static, some are useful in satisfying needs and others can be ignored. The useful ones (such as the parent), which provide comfort and pleasure, are experienced with a positive emotional charge; any that produce discomfort or pain are assigned a negative emotional charge. Things become confused when the same object (such as the parent) is ascribed with both kinds of charges, becoming both desired and feared. This is always the case when the object is alive and reactive, with a will of its own, as it is when it is a person or an animal. With such beings there is a real danger of being hurt. Transitional space that is filled with objects of desire also becomes land-mined with objects of fear; frequently, they are the same objects. It is no wonder that early in our lives, the issue of control is so important to our perceived survival.

At the same time as we are wrestling with sorting out our relationship to the many objects in our transitional space, we are having to determine how much of that space is inner and how much is outer. Where do I end and where does the other begin? How much of transitional space do I appropriate as myself? Where and how do I draw the boundary of my Self? Do I remain flexible and in touch with the objects in my world, or do I become overly defensive and build walls instead of boundaries? What is real and what is my imagination? What is the other really thinking and intending, and how much am I projecting upon the other, believing that I know what the other is thinking and intending? This issue is never ending and is the basis of most of the confusion that we create and experience throughout our lives.

Simply stated, we are all wrestling with transitional space, experiencing a gap between ourselves and others, between ourselves and inanimate objects, between ourselves and institutions (another form of objects), and most alarming of all, between the I and the Self. The latter gap is created by another act of objectification. One of our paramount projects in life is to become an individuated human through our relationships with the objects in our individual worlds. We can choose the extent to which we will objectify or humanize the objects in our personal worlds. To objectify an object is to ignore the living quality of it. We do this with generalizations (for example, "Everybody feels that way") and politicizations (for example, "All men are. . . ."). Life is acknowledged through the act of *personalization* (for example, "I feel this way"). This topic is further discussed in the next chapter, "Objectification."

The anxiety associated with the chaos of transitional space creates a need to organize and control that space. By doing so, we create meaning; this involves deciding on "right" and "wrong," "good" and "bad." In this way, morality is created to govern the interactions between the Self and others. At its root, morality serves to ensure the safety of the individual and the continuity of life of future generations; unfortunately, it tends to grow beyond its basic function, becoming codified and invested with a meaning beyond its function, as so frequently happens in the creation of religions. In this fashion cultures are formed, with individual pleasure being sacrificed to the continuation of group ideals. Acculturation is a gross act of objectification. Throughout history, millions of people have been killed in the service of cultures and moralities. The objectification of people (as "enemies," "infidels," or "barbarians") immediately robs them of life, so the actual killing of the body is only a small further step. That is why military training devotes so much effort to teaching soldiers how to depersonalize the "foe." A father of several children would find it difficult to kill another father of several children; it is easier for a "soldier" to kill an "enemy," a "conqueror" to kill a "native," a "defender of the faith" to kill a "heretic."

Because the chaos of inner space is closer to the Self, it is even more frightening than transitional space. Many impulses and feelings that arise from within (such as the desire to kill) are unacceptable to the Self. The convenient solution is for the Self to repress and deny such impulses, projecting them into transitional space, making the outer world even more terrifying than before. The usual repositories for such projections are people and "wild" animals—the objects that appear to have a will of their own, thus being less controllable. Most children begin to do this projecting at an early age; this explains why they cling and "make shy" in the presence of others. Security is to be found in the controllable objects such as mother, or inanimate things such as teddy bears and pacifiers. In the absence of effectively controlled objects in transitional space, the person is liable to experience symptoms of anxiety and possible panic attacks. One usually forgets that the source of fear is the unacceptable ("bad") impulses rising from within inner space, projected into transitional space. Without an object to project upon, the individual experiences general anxiety; objects that are projected upon become identified as the "enemy," or "wild" or "crazy." In addition to individuals, whole civilizations appear to need these objects of projection, even establishing permanent institutions to service them.

Thus, we create a gap between ourselves and others in transitional space. Whatever is unknown is interpreted as uncontrollable and thus viewed with suspicion, as a prospective enemy. In such a manner do many women and men, cultures and societies, religions and institutions view one another. Closer to home, this is the process by which children and parents become alienated and partners become separated. The gaps are maintained by the establishment of morality; somebody always needs to be "right," making others "wrong." Indeed, it is commonly known that, given the choice, most people would rather be "right" than happy. In such a way, grudges are held and punishments required. To surrender the gaps would mean giving up the convenience of having objects to project upon; then the individual would have to face the horror within, to own the unacceptable impulses and feelings that well up from inner space, and ultimately to be *responsible* for the Self. In the same manner, institutions could become responsible, rather than blaming and persecuting other institutions or individuals. The magnitude of the fear and anxiety that would accompany such responsibility explains why persons and institutions desperately cling to a rigid morality of rightness, making others wrong, instead of opting to let go of control and experience happiness.

The gap is usually only seen as a problem by the disenfranchised; it is frequently of little concern for those in power and control, who judge themselves to be "right." Banished from institutions and family, the disenfranchised are unable to participate in many decisions that affect their actions, their life-styles, and their livelihood. On the other hand, the institutions and family members who are in control lose the input of the disenfranchised, who, because of their "wildness," are frequently the most creative resources in society. But even worse is the tendency of the disenfranchised themselves to create an "enemy" of the institutions or family members in power, wasting much creative energy and resources in the maintenance of a feud. Frequently, the people who lose the most in such feuds are those not directly involved in it, rather than the embattled opponents. During marriage separations, the children usually suffer more than do the litigious parents. In the battle between institutions, the clients are deprived of a greater variety of services, many of which might be necessary for their health or happiness. In wars, often more civilians than soldiers are slaughtered.

Even more remarkable is the gap produced between the Self and the body. Because the Self is so identified with awareness and consciousness, it is usually thought to be the mind itself. Because so much that occurs within the body is unconscious and uncontrollable, the body too is relegated to a position outside of the Self in transitional space, and is related to as an object. Because our bodies are always with us, they become handy screens upon which we can project our anxieties, fears, anger, hate, and love. Thus, we make enemies of our bodies, disowning and being distant from them; and yet we could make friends with our bodies, owning and being intimate with them. The more alienated we are from our bodies, the more frightened and defended we become. The more split off from our bodies we become, the greater the distance across which we experience others. Thus, the gap widens.

Before the gap between the Self and others can be joined, a person must come to terms with the gap between the Self and the objectified Self. Such a healing within tends to accompany any bridging of the gap between the Self and others. It is tempting to believe that before you can love another, you must first learn how to love yourself, but it is more likely that you will learn to love yourself *while* you learn to love another. By bringing your Self forward and revealing your Self to another (an act of intimacy), you will discover how distant from others you have been, and how split off from your Self you have become. The awareness of those splits offers an opportunity to heal both gaps. Revealing the Self to others reveals the objectified Self to the Self; both the Self and other are recognized in such an intimate encounter.

The most primitive aspect of loving is "taking care of" the other; the infant desperately needs to be cared for, and the mother expresses her loving by taking care of the child. In a similar way, we take care of others, especially the helpless and the wild. By so doing, we can ignore our own inner "bad" senses of helplessness and wildness. The person in need of help faces issues of trust—can the other person be relied upon to deliver what is needed? Furthermore, the helped person comes under the control of the helpers, and thus, the helpers appropriate more transitional space to themselves. In keeping the other attached to the Self, we further objectify the other, and thus widen the gap. *Recognition* is an aspect of a more mature kind of loving; it acknowledges, respects, accepts and enlivens the life and uniqueness of the other. Because both parties are seen as able to take responsibility for themselves, the objectification inherent in taking care of another (doing and possessing) is abandoned. With such a kind of loving, we can more easily see that the gap is an unnecessary construction of our own. This increasingly felt sense of the assurance of the continuity of life is the development of faith—in one's own inner resources, in one's own location in the scheme of things, and in one's own existence in the face of nonexistence.

Once we recognize that the gap is of our own creation, and we acknowledge all the ways in which it has served us well, we can begin to become responsible for our own lives. Instead of being focused on the other across the gap—looking to see what the other can provide, how much the other can be trusted, or how dangerous the other might be—we can begin to have faith in ourselves as a full expression of life, complete in ourselves. We can then recognize and accept the existence of ourselves and others, being curious about each other's uniqueness, learning what we each can contribute toward the creation of a transitional space in which we all can flourish. We can then respect all beings and things, because when there is no gap, *they are us.*

*If all the beasts were gone, we would die from a great loneli-
ness of spirit, for whatever happens to the beast, happens to
us. All things are connected. Whatever befalls the earth,
befalls the children of the earth.*[1]

—Chief Sealth

Notes
1. M. Berman, *Coming to Our Senses* (New York: Bantam Books, 1990), 63.

OBJECTIFICATION

When children are born, they separate physically from their mothers. However, this physical separation is not accompanied by an immediate psychological separation. The newborn child is experientially and psychologically fused with its entire environment; everything is an extension of the child. Because the perceptual apparatus has not yet developed, early experiences are ill defined and all-or-none in their scope. The child experiences global reactions to hunger or satiety, heat or cold, pain or pleasure, dark or light.

As perception improves, children gradually begin to make out gross shapes around them and to attach labels to these shapes. They learn to distinguish one huge shape that comes and goes, seemingly associated with relief of distress; this shape they call "mother." Incidentally, "mother" refers to whoever functions as primary caregiver, male or female. In the first eighteen months of life, perceptual development involves a gradual naming of objects. By this naming, children are symbolizing experience and organizing their perceptions into a reproducible reality. In naming, children objectify the world around them. By this project of naming and distinguishing objects, which is necessary for their development, children learn to identify the world around them and begin to make sense of it, gradually establishing control over their surroundings. Objectification makes the world intelligible, reproducible, and subject to control.

Growing children move around in and play amidst this assemblage of objects. They make larger excursions away from their primary security objects, their mothers. As children crawl away, they look back over their shoulders, to make sure that their mothers are still there. As they become more confident, they will even play in the next room, with periodic voice contact with their mothers. Thus, children accumulate a built-up picture of their mothers, known as the "stable internal object" (see "Entitlement"). As this object becomes more stabilized, youngsters learn to move in the world with the security of knowing that their parents (and the protection associated with parents) exist. Thus, the symbolization of the other is a convenient method for psychological control and stability.

In the first two years, even as children are naming objects, they do not distinguish the objects as separate from themselves. The "mother" that comes and goes is experienced as an extension of the child. The teddy bear that the child holds is still part of the child, not a separate entity. Indeed, children see all things that they name and objectify as part of themselves; this is the "primary narcissism" of the infantile state. Although they are distinguishing separate objects (and thus honing their faculties of discrimination), they still see the objects as themselves. So, children have a me-mother, a me-toy, and me-food. Although the physical being separates from mother in delivery, the Self is not conceived until about age two—with a flash of *recognition* of the Self—and is delivered, about age three. When conception of the Self takes place, the child literally recognizes, "I am here!" (see above, "Nemo: The Abyss Within"). During the "terrible twos," children are experimenting with their self-directed wills and establishing a more stable experience of themselves. Sometime around three years of age, the Self is born with the establishment of self-awareness. From this point on, the person is no longer just a fixed biological entity; instead, the individual's will and personal choices come to the fore, and that individual can embark upon a life of individuation. As discussed above in the sections entitled "Strength and Power" and "Achievement or Mastery," the individuating person is capable of autonomous activity, living in strength, and self-awareness; this is in contrast to the person who individualizes, developing the False self, whose motif is power and who stands out rather than standing forth.

This has interesting ramifications for the development of relationships. As Becker described, parents are seen by their children as huge and powerful, protectors against the ravages of the universe.[1] Children experience gratitude, and feelings of security in having their parents on their side. However, the recognition slowly dawns that these parents, who are so powerful, could be a great threat to the children's well-being if ever they became displeased! An ambivalence resides in children, with the awareness that their parents, who are powerful enough to ward off the threats of the universe, could use this same power to destroy their children. Parents are larger than life, to be revered, appreciated, and feared. Thus, children learn to anticipate what the big people want, and devote themselves to the activities of pleasing in order to take control of the objectified others. Of course, children are terrified of being abandoned, and want control to assure themselves that they will not be left behind by their caregiver-objects. At first, this pleasing is quite primitive and impotent; the child learns to entice with crayon scribblings and peek-a-boo games. Very quickly, these activities become more sophisticated and are incorporated into a serious process of field-dependent pleasing, in which one's own experience is diminished in the face of the imagined demands of the external. A child establishes the Ideal self (walled Self) to try to get this control, to establish security against the Nemo. In this way, youngsters sell out the fledgling Authentic Self. If children choose a pattern of control and manipulation to develop a walled Self, then the Authentic Self, which at first exists only as a possibility, fails to germinate and develop. And so children become arrested in a world of objects, and deny their own autonomy and self-development in exchange for the security of control over the objects in their environment. Thus, no Authentic Self comes forth, and the individual does not learn to relate to the humanness of the other. This is the basis of the "I–It relationship" described by Buber.[2] For an "I–Thou relationship" to flower, individuals have to face the terror of nonbeing and accept aloneness and lack of control over external objects. In this way, truly personal relationships become possible.

Objectification, which was at first perceptual, is codified in language. We develop attitudes and beliefs about the objects around us, and relate to these concepts. This is the tyranny of the mind, which creates a world of symbols. Our language includes the assumption that the objects around us are real and need to be dominated. Also included in our language is a moral structure of right and wrong, appropriate and inappropriate, that helps to keep the individualizing person in line.

Children feel impotent amidst the objects around them; they seem like victims of size and development (and time!). Early childhood fantasies involve a reversal of power, where children become the center of activity, taking control of others. Listen to a young child playing with a doll or a truck, and you will see a fantasy of power and domination and control! The toys are externalizations of fantasied power reversal, which also occurs in dreams and imaginings of the future. "When I get big and you get little" precedes many youngsters' imaginings of what will ultimately unfold when they accumulate the power they crave. As well, these fantasies provide the matrix for life goals. Many of us have chosen occupations that are consistent with our early fantasies.

Children's dreams and fantasies are not physically experienced, as children lack the physical size and power to effect them. At puberty, the surge of sexual development provides an experience of life thrust in the body; for the first time, a physical experience of power is felt. This brings the possibility of dominating and controlling others. Often, this sexual power is associated with earlier unconscious fantasies, giving rise to the particular choice of sexual objects. The sexual charge involves a sexualized version of an early fantasied power theme, with its built-in reversal of earlier victimization. In the sexual charge, and choice of partner to dominate, there is a retelling of a life story (see below, "A Perspective on Sexuality"). We do not experience a sexual charge with everyone. There are thousands of components that go into making up the sexual charge (gender, age, size, shape, coloring, voice tone, attitudes, and other personality attributes). *We are not sexually attracted to a person; rather, we are attracted to an object* that most closely fits the elements in a now unconscious childhood fantasy. The elements in sexual attraction are the components of a power-and-domination theme looking for realization. We are not attracted to just anyone; we are attracted to someone who most closely fits the elements of the character in our fantasy that we require in order to compensate for earlier traumas. Thus, in every sexual charge there is a story; in the "microdot" is a condensed object-icon that contains elements from earlier life needing reparation.[3] In many ways, the sexual charge involves a revenge theme; we choose, not a person, but an object to dominate and control, to symbolically repair the problems of childhood powerlessness. This is "sex-on-the-brain." Although it is experienced physically as a charge, the phenomenon is mediated through the brain, in the unconscious fantasies of the cerebral cortex. This thesis denies the romantic myth that the sexual charge is for a distinct person. Indeed, the sexual charge is not personal at all; it has to do with the manipulation of a symbolized object that represents earlier unresolved incidents and traumas.

For an authentic relationship between persons, each would have to become aware of the objectification of the other, to acknowledge the objectification, and in this process accept it. This is the discipline involved in the practice of the communication model (see above: "A Model For Communication"). In relationships, we can share fantasies even when they involve objectifications of power. Indeed, we don't really usually relate to another person; we are generally relating to an object anyway. When we share our judgments, we are beginning to move through this objectification, to address the person of the other. Anything shared can enhance intimacy—and this includes sharing fantasies, judgments, and objectifications.

Objectification is a normal process, and is necessary for psychological development in earlier stages. Unfortunately, people tend to become fixated in this early stage of development, and the further possibilities of intimacy and revealing are blocked by fixed attitudes of objectification of one other. On the positive side, objectification helps to provide security in childhood, and later, generates excitement in the pursuit of power and sexual excitement.

Objectification is not bad; therefore, it is not necessary to stop it. Nevertheless, it is important to recognize the limitations of objectification. To provide security, social conventions, and day-to-day order, objectification is a very efficient human tool. However, in the domain of intimate relationships, this objectification must be acknowledged as one's own, not as the "truth." In this way, we can share our judgments (our objectifications) of each other. As in all other areas of relating, be aware, acknowledge the objectification, and in this way accept it. To own one's objectifications is to express more eros (life force); by denying objectifications, we continue to tie up life energy. To take one's objectifications seriously and believe they are "true" leads to death-in-life, with ever increasing objectifications. The Ideal self grows in power, and self-hate overcomes self-compassion; the world gets smaller, and *eros* succumbs to *thanatos* (the death impulse).

When one is responsible, acknowledging that "I am the one doing the objectification, to compensate for my fears," the Self establishes personal boundaries. With this acknowledgement, the individual experiences more fear but less objectification. Hence, the world of the Authentic Self opens up, yielding the possibility of authentic communication with the humanness of the other.

Neophytes often take this to mean a negation of objectifications—that they should be surgically removed. This amounts to a denial, which only delivers the Self into fixation without addressing the possibilities for further development. People can learn to play with romance and other objectifications without making them their ultimate meaning. In the same manner, they can play with sexual charges, which are based upon objectification, without making them the end-all. Enter the theatre, enjoy the movie, and then go back into the street to continue with life!

There is a spiritual dimension to this. In surrendering to objectifications, acknowledging them without resistance, people can die to the false ideas of themselves; they can then be reborn as Authentic Selves, who have learned to objectify in earlier stages of life and who can move through and beyond earlier restrictions, into genuine dialogue with other human beings.

Notes

1. E. Becker, *Denial of Death* (New York: The Free Press, 1973), 146.
2. M. Buber, *I and Thou* (New York: Charles Scribner's Sons, 1970), 11-12.
3. R. Stoller, *Sexual Excitement* (New York: Pantheon Books, 1979), 166.

Recommended Reading

Freud, S. *Civilization and its Discontents.* New York: W.W. Norton and Co., 1961.

Hycner, R. Between Person and Person: Toward a Dialogical Psychotherapy. *The Gestalt Journal,* 1988.

Lawrence, D.H. *Collected Poems.* New York: Penguin Books, 1977.

MORALITY

The child is born in "ontological anxiety" or "ontic anxiety"—the terror of nonbeing, which is at the root of our human nature. According to Paul Tillich, all other anxieties are varied expressions of this basic anxiety.[1] On the spiritual dimension, we experience anxiety in facing the inherent meaninglessness and emptiness of life. Most of us are too afraid to experience either the ontic or the spiritual dimension of our existence, and live most of our lives in the moral dimension. On the moral level, we exist in a tension between the absolutes of grace and condemnation; our day-to-day experience is one of guilt. In short, instead of facing the terror of nonbeing, or the emptiness and meaninglessness of life, we choose to live in the context of moral codes to cope with the basic anxiety.

Morality involves a system of right and wrong. Certain behaviors and attitudes are "right," and others are "wrong." We are "good" to the degree that we live within the "right" code, and "bad" when we live by the "bad" choices. As we can never fully live within these codes of behavior (or are afraid that we might slip), we live in a continual state of guilt. Whenever I say this is "true" or "false," or "right" or "wrong," I am exhibiting a moral stance. The moral position is depersonalizing; I am an object when I am either "good" or "bad"; I do not appreciate you the person when I say you are "right" or "wrong." To move into a personal intimacy, we must relinquish the temptation to see things in moral terms. Unfortunately, this will open us to the anxiety of our own emptiness, aloneness, and impotence. However, we also open up to our Authentic Selves.

The newborn infant is structured to function in a moral grid; the world of the infant is split into opposing poles of all or none, black or white, pleasure or pain, good or bad. Object relations theorists say that the child tends to experience one of these poles at a time, in all-or-nothing fashion.[2] "Good" describes the pleasure of a dry diaper, warmth, and satiety; "bad" applies to pain, hunger, and excess of cold or heat. In this context, everything is all-good or all-bad. The mother is all-good when she does the child's bidding, and all-bad when she does not. Children see themselves in this same light; they are either all good or all bad. Early on, children are fused with other people in their environment; hence, the Self–other symbiosis is experienced as either all good or all bad.

Children, as they learn to separate Self from other through the process of objectification, can label Self and other as good or bad. Hence, the mother might be good and the child bad (or vice versa). This paradigm is often replicated in interactions that come later, in adult relationships. When you disagree with me, I am inclined to think that I am all right and you are all wrong. This is just infantile thinking using a moral grid of good and bad.

Between the ages of two and three, the Self gradually "hatches" as a separate autonomous entity. With self-awareness come bodily feelings, and the development of the kinesthetic body, as described by Berman.[3] For the first time, children have the possibility of individual freedom and of realizing the Authentic Self, which has hitherto been present only as a seed principle. At this tender age, each of us has a major life choice to make. We can either face anxiety and separation, and surrender to life, or we can try to control the surroundings, to avoid the pain and anxiety of separation. Most children choose to control, to make the situation manageable, to overcome fear. And, of course, their parents also probably have opted for a life of conformity and individualizing; hence, children probably do not have a role model of an Authentic Self who is individuating in order to learn about being itself. Thus, people develop the walled Self via approval seeking, manipulation, external focus, and field dependency (see above, "Boundaries," "Strength and Power" and "The Ideal Self: Striving For Perfection"). At this stage of development, objects are seen as "not–I"; these objects must be controlled to protect the walled Self.

With the establishing of the walled Self (False self), morality becomes a convenient tool for providing a structure for behavior. Morality also gives a sense of security; all the child needs to learn are the appropriate behaviors to fit in, in order not to be abandoned. Thus, we have the intense potency of guilt and rules, and the strong inclination to be a "good boy" or a "good girl," even in adult years. Many dedicate their entire lifetime to living out the roles, rules, and conventions that are extrapolated to please the other. One chooses a life of convention and external orientation rather than developing the Authentic Self. One builds up a code of behavior to perpetuate this pleasing of the external, and tries to live up to this code, to survive. In this framework, *guilt* is important, to punish the Self when one transgresses this code of morality. Guilt is an internalized police structure, a way of keeping the False self in safety. No wonder we so readily want to feel guilty: we can feel the security of knowing we are paying for sins and thus won't be summarily turfed out from the kingdom!

The Ideal self is a product of morals—rules, prescriptions, and restrictions. The process of externalization in field dependency involves an abandonment of the Authentic Self in favor of the Ideal (False) self. Self-hatred is the price of this rejection of one's essential nature; power is the pay-off. Thus, the Ideal self functions with guilt and self-recrimination. Shame accompanies one's recognition of oneself. Shame, then, is an entrance to the

Authentic Self; in shame I am revealed as I am. Guilt operates against the revelation of the Authentic Self, and serves to perpetuate the masquerade of the Ideal self.

For many people who have lost touch with themselves, the path "home" is a process of becoming familiar with sensations and feelings *in the body* that either have not developed or have been forgotten. With this comes the delight of one's own feelings and awareness; however, one is also acutely aware of one's separation from other beings, and of the anxiety of nonbeing, ontic anxiety (see above, "Anxiety: Friend or Foe?"). I am autonomous, free, and capable of taking directed, intentional action in and on the world; unfortunately, I increasingly recognize that I am alone and face the dark dread of nonbeing. Strangely, the body has been seen as "bad," and we have been cut off from experience of our kinesthetic nature. We have to face guilt and anxiety to sink deeper into our own experience of our physical sensations and emotions.

Our society is held together by rules of "right" and "wrong"; laws represent a codification of morality, providing guidelines for appropriate behaviors and attitudes. This code of rules is not personal; we are not called forth as persons in the moral code, but only have to obey the convention. To become personal, one has to transform morality into personal situational ethics. When people begin to think for themselves and question laws, conventions, and established roles, they become alienated from the social order—they are more of their own Authentic Selves, questioning for themselves. However, they are less conditioned as moral beings.

This does not mean that an authentic person does not have principles. Indeed, such people, in dialogue with their surroundings, will constantly be making sensitive decisions based on personal ethics. To mature into the Authentic Self, they relinquish the easy, off-the-rack rules of conduct and replace them with situational ethics, where they are called upon to decide with their entire beings, using only the guidelines of their own personal conscience and code of honor. In short, personal ethics replaces morality when the Authentic Self comes into flower.

Religions generally have established codes of behavior, and hence are moral. Spirituality has to do with filling the emptiness and meaningless of life with our own personally felt meaning. Hence, spirituality is amoral and demands the presence of the authentic person.

Politicization involves a process of imposing one's morality upon other people. When an individual makes someone else "wrong," or blames them, this is politicization. When people share their feelings (positive or negative) and do not insist that the underlying judgments are "true," they are being personal. We have the option, in any interaction, of being personal or political. Whenever people insist that they are "right" (or "wrong," feeling guilty and blaming themselves), then they succumb to the moral. The moral can be a cowardly way of stepping back from life; to be personal involves courageously stepping forward into the unknown, responsively interacting with other people and with one's surroundings.

Blame operates against responsibly being oneself. When people blame others, or blame themselves in guilt, they are stepping back from life. When they accept others and themselves without having to force agreement, they can then step forth into life and engage in life-enhancing dialogue. To engage with another, they often have to relinquish their need to be "right." And of course, they want to be "right" so that they will not have to face the terror of nonbeing. Many political causes initially rooted in the feelings of individuals soon lose sight of the lives of other persons and are reduced to warlike fervor: where there could have been dialogue, joining, and learning, there is only blame and fault-finding. Righteousness is the enemy of life in the living moment. We lose ourselves and each other in trying to be "right." There is a tremendous arrogance in believing that I am "right," or that I know what is "true"; the arrogance of righteousness involves a tightness and a lack of acceptance that operates against vital dialogue. Righteous people generally have disdain for others who do not agree with them, believing them to be lesser, or simply wrong; in this disdain they move back from life, becoming prone to more illnesses and to less fulfilment.

People would usually rather be right than happy.

—Bennet Wong

Notes
1. P. Tillich, *The Courage to Be* (New Haven: Yale University Press, 1976).
2. D. Rinsley, "The Developmental Etiology of Borderline and Narcissistic Disorders," *Bulletin of the Menninger Clinic*, 44(2), 1980, 127–134.
3. M. Berman, *Coming to Our Senses* (New York: Bantam Books, 1990).

Recommended Reading
May, R. *The Meaning of Anxiety*. New York: Pocket Books, 1977.

DEVELOPMENTAL STAGES OF RELATIONSHIPS

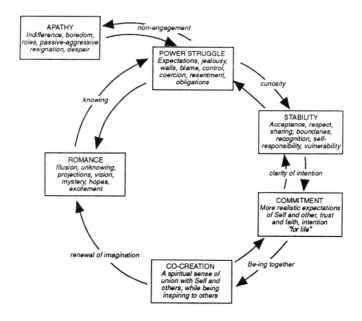

THE ROMANCE STAGE

At the beginning of a relationship each person is unknown to the other, and develops illusions that the other will satisfy his or her needs for security and meaning in life. The other is objectifed (that is, seen as an object, a role, a label or thing such as a "boyfriend" or a "business partner"). Onto the partner is projected an objectified version of what is hoped for and expected; the real person is unknown. On the positive side, there is also the stimulation of the imagination, a vision of what could ideally be possible. Mystery, excitement, anticipation, and hopes are all part of this stage, until knowledge of the other begins to develop. The romance stage can be one of "temporary insanity," with a loss of logic or reason, and can be maintained only by remaining ignorant of the real other.

THE POWER STRUGGLE STAGE

As the other becomes known and fails to measure up to expectations, resentment and blame build; each tries to bend the other to fit expectations through coercion, blame, and guilt, frequently by assuming a victim position. Walls (rather than boundaries) are built through pride and defensiveness. This is a stage of high energy, tension, arguments, hurt feelings, and excitement; in intimate personal relationships it is often expressed through sexual excitement. Jealousy results from a perceived threatened loss of the other, and is most frequently used to control the other's behavior. By struggling through differences and unmet expectations, each person will learn more about the Self as well as about the other. In order to resolve this stage, each of the parties must commit to remaining engaged in the struggle, with established guidelines (such as no violence or blackmail allowed). Each must learn how to share anger, rather than using anger as a means of control over the other.

If the struggle is not engaged, a passive-aggressive distance often grows, resulting in anxiety, depression, and often boredom and uncaring in a state of apathy (or indifference); in this way, the form of a "good" (apparently unconflicted) relationship might be maintained, although there will be limited intimacy and growth, increasing secrecy, and underlying resentments.

THE STABILITY STAGE

Stability (unlike apathy or indifference) results from a true recognition and acceptance of the other, with respect and support shown for the growth of each individual. People move out of the power struggle stage when they give up the need to be right, and begin to be curious about the process in which both of the parties are involved. Through dialogue, there occurs increasing revelation and vulnerability in both. Sharing stems from desire rather than obligation or expectation of return for investment. Individuality, creativity, fullness, a shared aliveness, and an interest in both the Self and the other are characteristics of this stage. Jealousy is shared as an expression of valuing rather than a means of controlling the other (as is the case in most relationships).

THE COMMITMENT STAGE

The commitment phase is marked by an expressed intention to remain with one another while each is exploring the more frightening and difficult (frequently childlike and early-family-related) personal issues. A deeper, new level of trust and intimacy develops. Expectations are now more realistic because the other is better known. Each is prepared to declare clear intentions in regard to the other. Commitments made in earlier stages may now have to be revised.

THE CO-CREATIVE STAGE

The understanding, love, growth, creativity, and knowledge that have been developed within the relationship now have inspirational effects upon others outside of the relationship, through the expanded sharing that is now possible. A spiritual sense of meaning and union characterizes this stage. Now there is a materialization and realization of what was imagined in the romance stage, albeit in a modified, more realistic form. In this, as in all the other stages, a new romance may develop and the cycle will renew itself.

Note that *these stages tend* to develop in a circular order, as illustrated in the diagram above; they can occur simultaneously and sometimes develop concurrently. Also, a person may be in romance with a baby while being in a power struggle with a partner. These stages can occur in all kinds of relationships: parent/child, husband/wife, business partners, friends and lovers.

Recommended Reading

Campbell, S. *The Couple's Journey.* San Luis Obispo, CA: Impact Publishers, 1980.

Campbell, S. *Beyond the Power Struggle.* San Luis Obispo, CA: Impact Publishers, 1984.

Intimacy

Intimacy is the condition of being known or familiar, one to the other, through a close personal connection or experience. In interpersonal relationships, such "knowing" of the Self by the other can occur in a number of ways. In usual circumstances, the Self is exposed to the other in a conscious act of *revelation*, offering the authentic nature of the Self to the other. Because the Authentic Self is usually so protected, such an offering is accompanied by an emotional state of vulnerability, an anxiety related to being exposed and possibly hurt. On a social level, the issue for the individual is fear of rejection; on a psychological level, it is fear of loss of ego boundaries (experienced as loss of independence); on an ontological level, it is fear of death of the Self.

The desire for intimacy and the motivation for offering the Self in face of such awesome hazards arise from a yearning for the experience of connection with another person. Such a condition aims to overcome a deep sense of loneliness and feelings of being invisible (unseen, or not understood), and possibly a conviction of worthlessness.

When another person has an interest in reciprocating that knowing, an atmosphere of trust and acceptance is fostered. This encourages further revelations, more vulnerability, and hence the development of an *intimate relationship*. When only one of the persons offers revelations and vulnerability (as occurs in traditional medical and religious practices), the other retains a position of power in such an *intimate state*. This is also the frequent situation in many interpersonal relationships (often interpreted as "one-sided" relationships), which tend to encourage more dependent and caretaking kinds of interactions, as with parents and authorities in social agencies.

In the intimate state, the individual feels *taken care of*; in an intimate relationship, the individual feels *cared about*. The intimate state generates issues of authority, dependence, obligation, possessiveness, jealousy, and privacy. The intimate relationship fosters self-development, growth, respect, acceptance, and responsibility.

The intimate state, as in the parent-child relationship, operates by the acceptance of roles and the fulfilment of obligations. Most children feel taken care of but not *known* by their parents. Many adult relationships are similar to the parent-child relationship. Such a state is frequently desired by both partners to the relationship, and often interpreted by them as being "intimate." With this situation, the personal Authentic Self is not exposed and the status quo is valued. Rules and obligations become a way of life, usually with the development of efficient roles and a sense of security.

In the intimate relationship, each person desires to expose the Self to the other and wishes to know the other, no matter how threatening that might be. With an open, honest revelation of the Self to the other, each person develops a knowledge of the Self while being vulnerable to the other. This is a person-to-person sharing, an "I–Thou" encounter in which both partners grow. Both persons are *responsible* for themselves, with an owning of all the feelings that might arise from such honest disclosing. There is no room for blame or victims. Value is placed on individual growth and respect for the other's Authentic Self. Sensitivity to the other and caring for what the other is experiencing are important elements of such a relationship.

Not all intimate situations are cooperative in nature; some are adversarial. For example, two athletes in competition can get to know one another intimately by studying and experiencing the other. War also can produce opponents with an intimate understanding of one another. Some interpersonal relationships maintain a level of excitement through challenge and control, developed through an appreciation of the other's strengths and weaknesses. In such intimate situations, although much is known about the other, little is revealed about the Self. Although there is a quality of closeness, the relationship is not intimate; revelation of the Self is a prerequisite of any intimate relationship.

Intimacy involves a *sharing*, in the spirit of desiring to know more about one another. Anything that is shared can serve to enhance intimacy. Sometimes, what is shared is a desire to help one another. It is important to be able to ask for help from the other, acknowledging the extent of helplessness. Such a "leaning" on the other operates against intimacy when it becomes a fixed pattern, an expectation that reduces a person's responsibility for the Self. It is important to be able to lean for a while, and not forever.

The question of power must be examined in all relationships. In the intimate state, the vulnerable person must rely on trust and self-assurance; the withholding person exercises control (often unconscious) over the other. In an intimate relationship in which both persons are vulnerable, one does not control the other; both have their own individual strength. For example, people often demand a change of behavior in the other in order to appease the hurt of jealousy. In an intimate relationship, sharing of hurt does not involve such control; sharing enables both to experience and appreciate the pain. The possibility exists that either or neither will alter their behavior. The total experience is shared by both.

The path of intimate relationship is not for everyone. Indeed, it may be inappropriate for many. The rewards include personal growth, the experiencing of authenticity and personal freedom, the sharing of aloneness, and a sense of fulfilment. The prerequisite is *courage* in two whole persons.

An intimate relationship is a loving shared by two solitudes.

—Jock McKeen and Bennet Wong

Loved
The path to healing is one which leads into discomfort
There is no easy way to open old wounds
 without allowing them to bleed
And pain is so often the price of awareness
 wisdom and love

Warriors may choose to walk alone
 experiencing life's dramas with power and fortitude
Crying in silence
 dying in isolation
They become the heroes — the glorified
 But rarely the loved

Love comes in sharing
 watching, feeling and allowing
 my pain to mix with yours
It is in these shared experiences I find my strength
 to face life's dramas
 with faith and confidence

For I am not alone
Your tears have become my strength,
 my courage to let go of my own
I treasure the tears we have shared
 just as I treasure our joy
It leads me down my path
 less afraid to bleed
Taking the steps to healing
 not dying in isolation

No hero
 worn and torn
—LOVED!!—

—Susan Clarke

Recommended Reading
Buber, M. *I and Thou.* New York: Charles Scribner's Sons, 1970.

MAINTAINING INTIMACY IN A RELATIONSHIP

Any relationship can be maintained from either a position of control or a position of vulnerability.

In a *power-based relationship*, each partner tries to maintain security by controlling the Self and the other. In the process, each plays a series of roles (good provider, competent mother, successful businessman, and so on). The Authentic Self becomes submerged beneath the myriad expectations of the security-based roles; the individual feels a sense of dullness or deadness. The roles are effective but depersonalizing. Although seemingly more secure, relationships based on power are accompanied by jealousy, anger, and anxiety when security is threatened.

The more one is prepared to share all aspects of one's inner world, including doubts, insecurities, pains, and fears, the more known to the other one can be. Revealing is the cornerstone of an intimate relationship. Through vulnerability—being revealed to one another—increasing awareness of the Self and the other becomes possible. The individuals in the relationship gain a sense of personal strength by revelation of the Authentic Self. Such a relationship is based on sharing of the Self rather than on need and security. This person-to-person dialogue fosters increasing recognition of each person. Each remains compassionate and sensitive to the feelings of the other, without rushing in to try to take them away. Thus, each partner is met with respect in a caring and sensitive manner, and can flourish in the dialogue of individuating separatenesses. Embarking upon such an intimate relationship can arouse anxiety, possibly excitement, and often fear of losing control. The rewards can be individuation for both parties, discovery of more of the authentic being, and a richer experience of life.

FACTORS IN CREATING AND MAINTAINING AN INTIMATE RELATIONSHIP

1. The welfare of the individual is more important than the welfare of the relationship. The relationship is not the goal; rather, it serves as a matrix for *individual growth*. The relationship is the garden; the individuals are the plants in that garden.
2. The goal of the relationship is for each person to *reveal the Self* to the other. In that revelation, one can discover more and more about the Self and the other. By moving out of roles, each becomes more individuated,

making possible an increasing person-to-person relationship. The individual moves from being invisible and unseen to being more visible and present, from *acting* in the world to *being* in the world.

3. The tools of revelation are *honesty* and *openness*. Both individuals must agree to reveal their processes, ideas, and feelings to the other as spontaneously and quickly as possible. When censorship of anything is judged to be necessary or desirable, this should be accepted; however, one should always immediately acknowledge the use of such censorship.

4. Both persons are fully *responsible* for themselves. One person cannot be blamed for the other's feeling; there are no victims in an intimate relationship. Although neither is responsible for the feelings and experience of the other, each can be sensitive to the other's pain, anger, jealousy, and sadness. Although one party does not cause the feelings of the other, each can have caring and compassion for the other's feelings. Neither person should be controlled by the feelings of the other.

5. When feelings are freely expressed and *shared without blame*, intimacy can develop. At first, it is often necessary for some feelings to be expressed with blame, in order to purge the energy that accompanies those feelings. After the blame is expressed, both persons can then reassess the interaction, and both can take responsibility for their individual parts in the interaction.

6. To maintain intimacy, feelings should *not be used for control*. A person's motives may be questioned by asking, "What is your intent in doing this?" It is important to check out suspicions, rather than assuming that they are a fact. For example, it is preferable to responsibly ask, "I feel controlled by your tears (anger, laughter, etc.); is this what you intend?" rather than "Your tears (anger, laughter, etc.) make me feel guilty!"

7. In a *primary* intimate relationship, each agrees that their relationship is the main focus of their intimacy. Intimacies shared with others would then be secondary to that primary relationship. Anything shared with others must be acknowledged in the primary intimate relationship, so that there are no pockets of experience that are not included in the primary relationship.

8. In establishing an intimate relationship, *many immature reactions and feelings* will emerge (such as jealousy, fear of abandonment, threatened loss of self-esteem, anger over unmet expectations). These can be shared in even their most unsavory forms (including blaming); in order to move toward intimacy, from controlling to sharing, both partners must then assume responsibility for their own responses and feelings.

9. *Any experience that is shared can enhance intimacy.* For example, anger, which is often used in more dependent relationships as a form of control, can be shared without blame in order to enhance intimacy. With vulnerability, one is continually being revealed to the other, and a mutual deep knowing of each other becomes possible.

10. *"Clearing"* is an important ingredient in the development and maintenance of this level of intimacy. Defenses and blockages will frequently emerge from one or both parties. The process of clearing, wherein each acknowledges judgments, feelings, and intentions, creates an atmosphere wherein each can be revealed without blame.

11. The *objectification* of the other is counterproductive if not shared. The tendency to objectify is a characteristics deeply rooted in the early development of the person. Examples of objectification include the tendency to view the other as a possession (as "my husband"), as an object of desire (as "my lover"), as a burden (as "my obligation"), or as a purpose (as "my reason to live") instead of as the person that he or she is. Revealing the process of objectification is an excellent way to personalize the other, moving closer as a result. At the same time, revealing objectification can be a source of excitement and challenge.

12. The relationship will encourage and nurture all experiences that are necessary to the *maturation* and fuller expression of each person. Frequently, what stimulates growth in one is threatening to the other. When one person is threatened, this can be shared without controlling the behavior of the other.

13. As intimacy deepens, both persons become more visible to themselves and to each other. There develops a quality of *presence*. Each person can agree to be as present as possible in the company of the other, sharing all feelings and thoughts.

14. *Expectations* of one another are not forbidden (contrary to some interpreters of the human potential movement). However, expectations should be fully revealed and agreed upon; if the agreement cannot be reached, this should be openly noted. Often, power struggles arise because one partner has an expectation that the other person has never agreed to meet; (s)he believes (s)he has the right to expect something of the other (entitlement), even without checking. We hold expectations to be of great value in an intimate relationship. Where little importance is attached to another, expectations can be quite low; whenever another becomes more important, expectations of that person will be raised. Meeting mutually agreed upon expectations can be a challenge to the growth and development of each person. However, it is important to remember that expectations should never be used for control; the other might voluntarily wish to live up to such expectations, but would have to freely do so, not through intimidation or threat. When one person decides not to live up to an expectation, some hurt may be experienced; in an intimate relationship, that hurt will be shared by both.

15. Each of us becomes defined as we set *boundaries* and limitations. Each becomes present and revealed as desires and expectations are expressed.

16. *Sexual charge* and intimacy are separate phenomena. Although they can be brought together in one relationship, there is a tendency for the

sexual charge to diminish as intimacy increases (see below, "A Perspective On Sexuality"). This can be a creative challenge for couples who wish to keep sexual excitement alive.

17. *Guilt* interrupts intimacy. Feeling guilty causes the person to withdraw from the contact boundary, indulging in self-recrimination.
18. *Pride* maintains distance; letting go of a prideful stance permits more intimacy.
19. Having to be *"right"* results in an invulnerability that is destructive to intimacy. Only when both parties can have their own unique points of view without one of them having to be "right" can intimacy flourish.
20. Whenever a conflict bogs down, either party can call *time out*, in which each can have breathing space without processing, in order to gain a more balanced perspective. When either calls time out, the request should be respected.
21. *Curiosity* facilitates intimacy. When both parties are curious, they can work through the prideful, righteous stances that keep them at a distance.
22. *Blame* kills intimacy. Whenever one person blames the other, no intimacy is possible.

Recommended Reading

Malone, T. and Malone, P. *The Art of Intimacy.* New York: Prentice-Hall, 1987.

The Developmental Stages of Loving

The three most confusing words in the English language are surely "I love you." The child who says, "I love you, mummy" cannot mean the same thing as the mother who responds with, "I love you too." Twenty years later, that same child who says to that same mother, "I love you, mother," has quite a different picture of what that now means. Undoubtedly, mother's response, using the same words, now means something different than it did twenty years previously. What has changed?

A young woman's "I love you" directed to her father has a considerably different meaning than those same words directed to her husband. Aside from the obviously different sexual connotations, there are usually other qualitative differences between these two. What is even more confusing is that twenty years later, those same words expressed by that same woman to that same husband now can have an entirely different overlay of meaning. Sometimes, each of the parties is unaware that the other attaches a different meaning to the phrase. Yet the words remain the same. What, then, has changed?

A man says, "I love you" to his lover; a child says the same to a pet cat or a doll; the same words are used between friends. During the seventies, flower children said the phrase to everybody, even their enemies; now that they are older, a majority of the flower children have become like their previous enemies, and their expression of love has taken on a different meaning. Christians are exhorted to love others as themselves, which is easy to do until their own lives or livelihood is threatened; then the words "I love you" seem more fitting to intimate situations. Again, the words remain the same. What has really changed?

In all of the above instances, although the words "I love you" remain constant, the *meaning* is different in each situation. Most people are confused by the many faces of love; the word "love" is used with different meanings in different contexts. Furthermore, with time, although the situation may remain fairly consistent, each person is likely to change. With changing needs, increasing maturity and understanding, heightened awareness and more experience, the meaning a person attaches to such words as "love," "independence," "need," and "commitment" changes.

A person grows through a process of change—physically, emotionally, mentally, and spiritually—and so the meanings of words will change within each individual; like people, words are in the process of change. If we are ever to really be able to communicate with one another, we must understand and accept that process. Because love is recognized as one of the most essential of feelings that we communicate to one another, we must recognize the stages that the meaning of the word "love" passes through, reflecting the stages that we as individuals are passing through. The meaning of "love" changes as the person changes and grows.

Much confusion arises from seeing *love as a commodity*, something that can be exchanged in transactions. In this economic approach, a person has only so much love to give and must be a shrewd investor in order to ensure a healthy return on an investment in another person. Both parties can become adversaries who have to proceed with great caution. Love in this bartering sense can often lead to mistrust and conflict. Both parties in the transaction become bound rather than freed.

Children are often viewed as empty vessels that must be filled up with love so that they can later give this love away to other people. According to this view, people are depleted of love and need to refuel from someone else. Parents, children, and lovers all become fixed in the pattern of exchanging love as if it were an object, a commodity that can be used for control of one another.

If we manage to move beyond the restrictive concept of love as a currency, we can begin to see a dynamic quality to loving. When love is more of a state than a commodity, the lover and the beloved are immediately freed from dependency and the fear of loss. From a dynamic view, loving is a *feeling in action*, moving both to others and to the Self. It is a natural function of being human, and although it is most easily recognized when there is an object of the loving, an object is not necessary; it is possible to just exist in a state of loving. Even if there is an object of loving, the love need not be returned. However, most people choose to see objects of their loving in the manner of an investment; most fears about loving come from that common attitude, and vulnerability then becomes an issue. The pain of loving often occurs when one's expectations that the love will be returned are not realized.

People are capable of being loving, of being able to choose the object of their loving, or having no object at all. All choices are based on individual factors. Commonly, those factors are neurotic in nature, that is, attempting to fulfil unmet needs from early developmental history, similar to our motivation in most of our relationships. It is possible to go beyond those needs to create a state of loving. Some people advocate a *transcendental* approach (i.e., going beyond the Self) to accomplish this. We believe that it makes more sense to remain human and emotionally involved in a personal growth project, so we advocate a *transformational* approach (i.e., changing the form of expression of the Self). Neither is right; one's approach is a matter of personal choice (see above, "Is Change Possible?").

The loving state is a state of *transparency*, without defense or covert intention. Being loving calls forth the Authentic Self, which is exposed even though it may invite rejection or judgments from others. Such revelations are more easily shared with others who value the person as (s)he is, not as someone to meet their expectations. When that other person returns loving with his or her own revelatory loving, there develops a loving relationship.

Each of us always benefits from our loving, whether of the other or of the Self. The other person can choose to benefit in whatever ways are deemed suitable. We believe that the highest benefit comes from returning that loving with similar self-revelatory loving; authenticity invites authenticity. Only by so doing can a person really grow.

Love is not a thing, object, or noun; it is an action, a verb, involving emotions. It is the moving *energy of union*, involving an empathetic process, in a live state of being. Through loving, we are able to locate ourselves in the scheme of things; it is a way of lighting and revealing the Authentic Self both to the Self and to the other. Each person experiences loving as a process, in a variety of ways and on many possible levels, the earlier ways remaining as felt possibilities even as the person progresses in age and experience. The following ways are arranged in rough order according to the maturational process; they are cumulative but not necessarily serial in nature.

1. LOVING IS SUPPORTIVE

At birth, helpless, dependent children feel loved as they are taken care of. This supportive aspect of loving is the earliest one experienced (as security) by each person. Because the infant would perish without such support, this first stage of loving is associated with insecurity. For the rest of their lives people will carry the remnants of that insecurity, even though they will most likely grow into reasonably self-reliant persons capable of looking after themselves. Deep down inside there remains the fear of being abandoned (death), for which being loved offers some temporary relief. A person arrested in development at this stage will be emotionally field dependent, requiring the approval of others and needing to be needed by others. Often, on the positive side, such people become caretakers and religious or political leaders; on the negative side, they can become socially, emotionally, and medically helpless. Characteristically, they become placating, manipulating, controlling, and sometimes openly threatening. Loving, supportive people (both positive and negative) need one another to find security and meaning in life.

2. LOVING IS EMPOWERING

As children mature, they become interested in mastery of their own life, beginning with crawling, walking, and talking. As they experiment with these skills, they constantly monitor their parents' reactions, seeking approval for their newly discovered independence. If the parents have a need to be needed, such actions will be subtly discouraged (for example, in overprotectiveness). The "good enough" parent will encourage a child's ever-increasing steps toward independence and autonomy. Similarly, in adulthood, loving persons take pleasure in witnessing their loved ones becoming more of themselves as persons, full of their own strength and less needy of the approval of others.

3. LOVING IS ENLIGHTENING

Every person's growth as an individual (individuation) involves an ever-increasing awareness and knowledge of the Self. Loving promotes that kind of learning, providing the information, the experiences, the encouragement, and the feedback in a caring way. Too often, feedback is not provided lovingly; it can be critical, disapproving, and controlling, fostering compliance and impairing the person's self-esteem.

4. LOVING IS RECOGNIZING AND VALUING THE PERSON

Loving sees the other as an autonomous being, separate and whole, *not* as a possession or an object. Unfortunately, most children are raised in objectified roles (good sons, successful students, loving daughters) without much experience of being valued for the persons they are. Thus, they will tend to objectify themselves and lose touch with the Authentic Self, which would be supported by high self-esteem. In loving recognition, the being of the person is witnessed by the other; thus, the Self is known.

5. LOVING IS PLEASURING

Loving takes pleasure in the pleasure of the other, takes delight in witnessing the spark of life that is ignited in the joy of the other. It does not cause that pleasure in the other; that would be control. It contributes to the situation in which the other finds delight. *The pleasure is in the loving*, in experiencing the exhilaration of loving.

6. LOVING IS VULNERABLE

During the developmental years, the majority of one's experiences prepare one for security and survival. Promoted through education are such defenses as roles, achievements, and compliance. Etiquette and morality are taught in the home and at church. Each person learns how to control emotions, overcome impulsiveness, and manipulate others. These are all necessary to the person's success as a responsible member of society, but the Authentic Self tends to become trapped by these conventions. In intimacy, the person desires to share that Self with the other, to become recognized by the other, but can do so only by shedding those defenses (by now a difficult task) and presenting that Authentic Self in a vulnerable (defenseless) way. This is risky and often anxiety-provoking, but to do so is an essential aspect of loving. Without vulnerability, relationships become entombed in roles and the persons remain unknown to one another. Personal growth is possible only through vulnerability; loving offers recognition.

7. LOVING IS SHARING

Between people, whatever is shared enhances intimacy. To be loving is to offer to share whoever and whatever we are and whatever we do, our own space and time, our knowledge and understandings, our histories and experiences, our concerns and personal hurts, our fears and excitements, our possessions and our needs, our sadness and joy. The more we do so, the more of ourselves we reveal and know. Even anger can be shared to enhance intimacy, when it is given boundaries and not used to threaten and control the other (as is too often the case). When persons share in this way, they express more of themselves and become more individuated through establishing an *interdependence*. When sharing is impaired, as it is in most families, the children have a need to rebel to become independent and individualized, but not individuated. Sharing helps to establish boundaries and autonomy, but caretaking and obligations establish dependency and walls.

8. LOVING IS CO-CREATING

When loving is shared, a *spiritual bond* is experienced, and in this state of mutual sharing, caring, and revelation all persons become more of themselves, more authentic and more fully present to one another. In this loving state, people emit an energy of wholeness, light, and peace that is easily discernible to others. Such people live their lives in co-creative projects that share their loving with others in society in inspirational ways.

9. LOVING IS ETERNAL

Persons who love and are loved become part of a dynamic relationship in which each is *transformed*. The presence of each is indelibly etched in the ever-developing pattern of the other, and can never be removed. The essence of what has been involved in loving is forever.

What thou lovest well remains, the rest is dross.[1]

—Ezra Pound

Notes
1. E. Pound, "Cantos" (1925-1959) LXXXI, in *Bartlett's Familiar Quotations*, 15th ed., edited by J. Bartlett (Boston: Little, Brown and Co., 1980), 792.

Recommended Reading
Buscaglia, L. *Love*. Greenwich, CT: Fawcett Crest, 1972.
Fromm, E. *The Art of Loving*. New York: Harper and Row, 1962.

A Perspective on Sexuality

Much confusion exists in relationship to sexuality—because the subject is emotionally highly charged, because of lack of agreement on definition of terms, and because of a scarcity of well-researched knowledge about the subject. In our presentations about sexuality, we commonly note that most people have become fixed on one or a few aspects of the subject, reflecting a deeply personal bias for or against a particular point; they then stop hearing or recognizing the whole picture that is being addressed. Although sexuality is broken down into several component parts for the sake of discussion, it is important not to lose sight of the overall perspective.

The first major area of confusion lies in the use of the word "intimacy" as a euphemism for "sexual intercourse." When a person refers to an "intimate relationship" with another, what is usually meant is a sexual relationship. Throughout this book, the word "intimacy" is used specifically to represent the state of vulnerability, openness, and sharing that can exist between two people. A sexual experience can be intimate, but, in our findings with people, more often than not it is the opposite. In our view, *sexual excitement and intimacy are separate phenomena*; they do not naturally or readily fit together. Indeed, in common experience they tend to work against each other: as intimacy develops, sexual excitement tends to diminish.

THE ROMANCE OF SEXUALITY

The most exciting time in a relationship is often the beginning period, when not much is known about one another but much is imagined. Each person's dreams, fantasies, and hopes for the future contribute to his or her *romantic* vision. This vision is highly personal, containing within it a person's past history and life experiences, bad as well as good. Much is projected upon the other, with the exciting prospect that, at last, the romantic vision will become a reality. The concomitant anxiety that it will not become a reality, or that rejection is a definite possibility, serves to heighten the excitement. The anticipation is that the sexual experience will be the ultimate expression of that romance. When one person's romance fits the other's, the relationship becomes truly romantic; when it does not, the relationship ends in tragedy— a tragic romance.

THE END OF ROMANCE

Given two people who have discovered mutually satisfying romantic visions and enjoy a relationship that finds expression in shared sexual excitement, what could possibly go wrong? In North American society most couples come together in this romantic fashion. Within five years the majority of those relationships have ended in separation or divorce. In most instances, these endings are accompanied by bitterness, anger, depression, and feelings of failure and low self-esteem. For many, the intrusion of reality destroys the initial flush of romance. As each person becomes familiar with the other and the other person becomes known (an important aspect of intimacy), it becomes difficult and then impossible to fit that person into the romantic role that was expected. Although the possibility of intimacy between the two has increased, most people tend not to value that possibility. Instead, the focus is generally on the excitement, the romance, the thrill, without which, for most, the relationship dies.

Obviously, romance and reality tend to be mutually exclusive—one destroys the other. Given our definition of intimacy as the expression of shared authenticity (the reality of the person), it seems that romance and intimacy are also mutually exclusive. Because sexual excitement is often based on romance, is it possible that sexual excitement and intimacy are also mutually exclusive? That proposal deserves further consideration. Consider the following:

> DON JUAN: Do my sex the justice to admit, señora, that we have always recognized that the sex relation is not a personal or friendly relation at all.

> ANA: Not a personal relation! What relation is more personal? More sacred? More holy?

> DON JUAN: Sacred and holy, if you like, Ana, but not personally friendly. Your relation to God is sacred and holy; dare you call it personally friendly? In the sex relation the universal creative energy, of which the parties are both helpless agents, overrides and sweeps away all personal considerations, and dispenses with all personal relations.[1]

CATEGORIZING SEXUALITY

For the sake of discussion, the large topic of sexuality will be considered under the following four headings: the biological aspects of sexuality, sensual erotic sexuality, the sexual charge (including the sexual charge of pornography), and the transpersonal dimensions of sexuality.

Dimensions of Sexuality			
Biological	*Sensual-Erotic*	*Sexual Charge*	*Transpersonal*
Physical	Physical	Mental	Spiritual
Tension	Tension	Emotional	Meaningfulness
Endocrine	Parasympathetic System	Sympathetic System	The Higher Self
Neuroendocrine	Diencephalic	Cortical	
Orgasmic	Stroking	Penetration/ Fenestration	Ecstasy
Reproduction	Pleasure/Pain	Domination/ Submission	Union
Organic	Sensory	Symbolic	Ineffable (Inarticulate)
Impersonal	Impersonal	Impersonal	Impersonal

BIOLOGICAL ASPECTS OF SEXUALITY

The biological aspects of sexuality are generally taken for granted, even though there are many gaps in our knowledge of this very important subject. It is assumed that the sexual drive is biologically determined, mediated by a complex neurohormonal network that affects the mechanisms of behavior. Simply stated, the assumption is that each of us is genetically patterned to produce the appropriate hormones to prepare our body for its characteristic sexual functioning and behavior, and then to drive us toward consummation of that behavior in the act of sexual intercourse with a person of the opposite sex. The *telos*, or purpose, of this is of course continuation of the species.

If the above assumption is correct, the natural history of sexual behavior would go something like the following. The male animal has a relatively stable hormonal balance, offering a preparedness for but not a drive toward sexual activity (contrary to popular belief). The female of the species has a complex, rhythmic cycle of events occurring within, a delicate orchestration of hormonal balances. When uninhibited, ovulation occurs approximately once a month. In order to enhance the chances of fertilization of the ovum at that time, a complex, subtle intoxicant (a pheromone) is emitted into the atmosphere, which, if it makes contact with the male, will stimulate his sexual neurohormonal apparatus. Sexual intercourse would be the result— but only once a month! This is what we refer to as "natural" (i.e., according to nature) sexuality, determined by our biology. From this point of view, all other sexual behavior is considered "unnatural" or "perverse" (because its aim is something other than reproduction). Some religions have made a moral code of this kind of sexuality, claiming that only what is "natural" is "moral"; usually, the logic is not carried to its "natural" conclusion (making all sexual intercourse other than at the time of ovulation immoral). Obviously, biological sexuality involves pre-human drives, and hence is not personal to the individual.

THE SENSUAL-EROTIC

The next level of sexual interest occurs at the neuronal level. The body's neurological system is excited by different stimuli, providing a wide variety of pleasant and unpleasant experiences. Some specific areas (the erogenous zones), when touched or stroked in particular ways, stimulate within the person an excitement or arousal that is described as "sexual." More specifically, *it is a sensual arousal to which sexual meanings are attached*. The arousal of the senses through touch (stroking, texture, warmth, and so on) is only one of many possible perceptual arousals; for example, arousal is possible through vision (colour, form, size, darkness), hearing (music, sounds of breathing, silence), smell (body odours, perfumes), and taste (body tastes, food, drinks). Such arousal through sensual stimulation constitutes the erotic aspect of sexuality. This is mediated through the parasympathetic nervous system, which produces relaxation and a general feeling of well-being.

The sensual-erotic aspect of sexuality is valued to varying degrees by different people. To some, it is the most important aspect of sexuality; to others, it is only the means to a more exciting end. A wide variety of tactile stimuli can be eroticized, ranging on a pleasure-pain continuum from tender caresses and gentle massage all the way to rough handling, pinching, biting, and hitting. The characteristic pattern of western civilization is gentle caressing and stroking. The arousal of the body by stroking is not necessarily related to any specific person or object; stroking of the body is in itself all that is necessary to produce the pleasant, erotic experience. In this way, the sensual-erotic is essentially impersonal; the specific person that provides that stroking is secondary.

Sensual-erotic experiences are basically physical, mediated through the neurological sensory apparatus. In the brain, the centers chiefly responsible for integration and experiencing of the stimuli are in the diencephalon, which functions below the level of the thinking brain. Such experiences are basic to all higher animals, not only humans; this fact is evidence that they are "naturalistic" and impersonal.

THE SEXUAL CHARGE

The sensual-erotic experience tends to be soft and rounded, but there is another kind of sexual experience that is sharper, more highly charged, more acute and immediate, more urgent and driven. Sexual excitement is mediated through the sympathetic nervous system (which has been described as the "fight/flight/fright" system). The sexually charged experience is impersonal—the object of the charge can be anyone or anything selected by the individual. The specific person is secondary, as in the sensual-erotic experience. Unlike the sensual-erotic, which is biological and sensory, the sexually charged experience is primarily stimulated by *symbols*. It is mostly a mental process involving the cerebral cortex, which operates with the symbolic. Objects (including language and objectified people) are assigned specific meanings that are then tied to specific and highly personalized feelings. The process of symbolization is important to the development of civilization and its culture. At the same time, however, it tends to turn us away from our natural roots and tendencies. It is a learned process, determined by the interaction of the individual with the culture.

At the level of the symbolic, sexually charged form of sexual excitement, each individual reflects a combination of influences involving the culture (the cultural romance) and his or her personal history. From an existential point of view, underlying both of these influences are unresolved childhood issues: an ongoing fear of helplessness and annihilation, feelings of worthlessness and self-doubt, and, ultimately, a fear of abandonment by others that (for the infant) leads to death. The solution offered by society is for each individual to master survival skills and to control the environment, especially the people in that environment, making them predictable. The individual is caught in a struggle for power. At the same time that one wants to control others, there is a desire to submit, to give over and have someone else take charge. This craving for domination/submission becomes the main theme that is brought to sexual experience at the symbolic level. It is what fires the excitement for the sexual charge.

The chief means of expressing the domination/submission theme in sexuality is through sexual intercourse. The desire is for either penetration or fenestration (being entered or penetrated), which are opposite sides of the same coin. The underlying theme is control—both the dominator and the submittor feel triumphant in being strongly desired and needed by the other. Both feel validated and temporarily lose their fear of abandonment. To varying degrees, all interaction between people can be seen as embodying this domination/submission theme. There is a sexually charged excitement in the pursuit of a loved object in the romantic stage of any sexual relationship, on the dance floor or at a cocktail party. There is the thrill of domination when the other person fully agrees, verbally or behaviorally, to do one's bidding. The possibility of failure, of being rejected, only serves to heighten the excitement. There is equal power in submission; many people experience a thrill in being the object of desire or of domination. After a time, there is a lessening of the excitement when the surrender and domination have become commonplace and taken for granted, as will happen in the majority of committed relationships within five years.

Sex is engaging in the first rounds; what sustains interest in the long run is power.[2]

—Madam Jiang Qing

THE SEXUAL CHARGE OF PORNOGRAPHY

In the domination/submission theme there is always a victim. Depending upon one's point of view, the victim is either the dominator or the submittor; actually, (s)he is both! All pornography graphically expresses that theme. Because most men are primarily visual in their sexual stimulation, the theme is presented via the ambience of the poses so readily found in pornographic magazines. Each posed model, through the positioning of the body and the look in the eye, offers both an invitation and a challenge. It is a good question to wonder who is the victim and who is in control—the model in the magazine, or the person who is driven to buy and view the pictures. All sexually charged excitement carries this pornographic theme, even though morality often tries to deny and camouflage it. In its extreme, the domination theme is present in child pornography—who could be more submissive than a young child? For most women (whose sexual charge tends to be less visually oriented than men's), the theme runs through all of the Harlequin Romances in which the sweet young woman heroine typically tames and captures the wild, unmanageable hero. Rather than being stimulated by pictures, most women (though not all) are charged with the fantasy of the domination/control plot or story. Both men and women crave to capture the consciousness (attention) of the other.

TRANSPERSONAL DIMENSIONS OF SEXUALITY

Experiencing a deep sense of loneliness, most people desperately attempt to join with the other at all levels of interpersonal relationships, including the sexual. If such is the ambition, acts of domination/submission are doomed to endless repetition in the attempt to succeed.[3] Only through recognition of the other (the truly personal experience), and recognition of the union that already exists with the other, can the authentic transpersonal situation be entered. Through deeply intimate sexual experiences, the individual surrenders the Self, experiencing beyond the Self a unification with the rest of the universe. It is not just a joining with the other; it is recognition of the state of being already joined with the other. To experience that sexually requires moving beyond the fear of aloneness and coming to terms with the fear of death. Such sexual experiences involve a true letting go, a *surrender* of the

Self (not to the other, as in the case of submission related to domination), a preparedness to die in the arms of the other. The person dies and is reborn: in such an act is contained the *divine*, the *state of grace*. This dimension of sexuality involves letting go of the individual Self; hence, transpersonal sexuality is not personal.

CONCLUSION

What is called sexuality can be seen to be much more complex than is usually assumed. All sexual experiences carry with them elements of a great variety of levels that we have arbitrarily divided into four. Each person individually values the various levels, and operates within them in a unique, idiosyncratic manner; hence, the term "sexuality" describes a highly individual aspect of people. From this point of view, there is no sexual pathology, only individual uniqueness. Each person expresses sexual preferences, excitements, and practices that reflect the individual's underlying life themes. Sexuality is the personal diary of each person's history, containing all the hopes and fears, the fantasies and experiences, the very meaning of that person's existence. It is no wonder that one's sexuality is so carefully guarded, even from one's self-awareness.

With the understanding that there is no pathology, provided there is consent between partners, it could be concluded that sex therapy is unnecessary. Certainly that is our belief, given the philosophies of sexual therapy that currently dominate the field. Sex therapists today are much too mechanical in their ideas, advocating exercises and practices that would promote easier and more effective functioning of the sexual apparatus: the attitude seems to be that we should provide an oil and lubricant job for the human body as we do for our automobiles. What is missing is appreciation of the *meaning* of individual sexuality at all levels. Often what is needed is for an understanding facilitator to pique the person's curiosity about the deeper meanings of personal activities.

What becomes obvious is that at these levels, the sexual experience is chiefly impersonal. The challenge in ongoing relationships is to uncover the sources of excitement and then bring these into the intimate sharing of the relationship. This project, making personal the impersonal, begs for further exploration. From this point of view, sex "therapy" is unnecessary. What is desirable is self-awareness, with appreciation of those levels of meaning for the person. Removed from the moral perspective, no act or desire is intrinsically wrong; what can be faulted is insensitive expression of a particular desire. The important word is *consent*: for growth and mutual benefit to occur, the participants in the relationship must agree on each aspect of the interaction. To transgress consent and personal boundaries converts the sexual experience into an act of violence (as in rape). Each person should be able to explore the meaning of particular desires and impulses in a context where no one is disadvantaged.

With the mutual sharing of the underlying sources of excitement, each person becomes more vulnerable and known to the other, enhancing intimacy. Unfortunately, as this happens, much of the domination/submission factors involved in sexual excitement tend to disappear and excitement tends to diminish. Instead, sexual experiences become more fulfilling, which for some (especially women) has an excitement of its own. It could be described as an "intimacy charge" related more to excitement over surrendering than to submitting. Such people may describe this as their sexual excitement, and be happy with it. Those who are obsessed with domination/submission (especially men) might become dissatisfied with the loss of such a charge and feel a need to seek therapy or change partners. If they want to recover that form of excitement in their relationship, they will need to explore creative ways of rediscovering the domination/submission themes in their relationship. Fantasy, play-acting, stimulation of the senses, and exploration of pornographic stories and movies are all possible approaches. Seeking experiences outside of the relationship is a common solution, but because of the threat to the primary relationship, it is a risky one, and not recommended.

By incorporating the understandings in this section into an intimate, caring relationship, it is possible that each person will experience more freedom in exploring all the dimensions of being involved in sexuality, ranging from the profane to the divine. With this exploration may come growth, self-discovery, appreciation of the Self and the other, an ever-growing intimacy, and most of all, a greater sense of meaning in life!

Notes
1. G.B. Shaw, *Man and Superman* (Baltimore: Penguin Books, 1952), 163.
2. Madam Jiang Qing, quoted in *Time* March 21, 1977.
3. J. M. Russell, "Sartre's Theory of Sexuality," in *Journal of Humanistic Psychology*, 19 (2), Spring 1979, 41.

Recommended Reading
Stoller, R. *Sexual Excitement.* New York: Pantheon, 1979.
Sartre, J.-P. *Being and Nothingness.* New York: Washington Square Press, 1966.

Empathy, Resonance and Energy

According to Webster, empathy is "the imaginative projection of one's own consciousness into another being."[1] In practice, we tend to believe that empathy is a person's capacity to actually feel another person's feeling, much as understanding is a person's ability to know another person's ideas. Frequently, some reference is made to an ability to feel another person's "vibes" (vibrations), suggesting some form of energy transfer; angry emotions, for example, produce a form of energy vibration that can be detected by another person. It is believed that because of such energy vibrations we have an effect upon the lives of others, and bear some responsibility for their emotional lives. A common belief is that some people's energy is "toxic" and should be avoided, and the energy of others is "nutritive." Such a belief presupposes a view of life in which the Self is a victim to others and circumstances rather than the creator of experience.

The human body creates energy through the metabolic process of digesting. That energy is used for all of a human being's experiences, including emotions. This is the energy that most assume is able to influence and control others; the greater the energy, the more powerful the person, behavior, or feeling. Sensitivity, the ability to feel what the other person feels, is a receptive rather than a transmissive function of that same energy. It is as though we are radio receivers in the midst of a huge number of transmitted energy vibrations, vulnerable to their influences. Such a metaphor supports the concept of field dependence.

For a moment, imagine that there is only one energy, a cosmic energy flowing through the universe. Imagine that this energy is appropriated at the point of conception of each person, and is organized by developing human beings for their own use, all the while remaining in the constant cosmic flow. The body's metabolic processes are the means of utilizing that energy for the developing person; the energy is not created, it is *organized*. It is not the body's own energy. We all swim in the same energy pool, which is shared by all of us; in this way, we always remain connected with one another at a deep energy level. What appears to be unique to a person are the attributes given at the time of conception plus all of the energy blocks and resistances (Reich's "character armour"[2]) that we develop in our experiences within our family and society. If all of these energy blocks and resistances were eliminated (as some spiritual practices and religions propose), the Self would disappear in a "peak" transpersonal experience of oneness, revealing the basic unity of cosmic energy.

In this concept of cosmic consciousness, separation is seen as an illusion based on the defenses of the ego. It is this illusory ego that is supposed to create, transmit, and receive energy vibrations; it is thought to have the power to influence and affect other people, to be able to "know," across a gap, what is happening in the world of another person. The gap is crossed through empathy and understanding, which would require some energy transfer. Such activity would tend to result in an energy loss or drain; this is often reported by counsellors, who "burn out."

Suppose that there is no energy transfer, but rather, that energy is in constant flow among all things and all people, blocked only by individual or group resistances, which have mostly been developed out of fear or hurt. When a person hurts, other people, who are always connected at a deep level, will feel their own hurt *in resonance* with the suffering individual. In similar fashion, there would be no understanding of the other, only a felt experience of understanding the Self as it is able to resonate *in relationship* to the other. This would be true "recognition" (which word, as we saw above, is from the Latin root *re + cognoscere:* to know again, to be reminded of something about the Self connected to the other). In this situation, the Self is stimulated to resonate and release static blocks to energy flow. Being free of the power motivation to take care of the other, or to push the other to change, or to escape the influence of the other, the Self does not lose energy; instead, energy is set into motion within the Self as a resonance, which is experienced as a sense of aliveness, fullness, and movement. Instead of experiencing "burn-out," persons undergoing resonance would feel more energetic and would know themselves all the more. Because the energy is not their own, but rather is the expression of the infinite cosmic energy, it is always available. Energy is never lost, only displaced.

Having lost the sense of connection with oneself and with others, most people have opted for a power mode of relating, taking care of one another's welfare and feelings. They metabolize energy in order to move about people and things in the field, to ensure their own safety. Life takes on all the attributes of obligations and roles, made possible only by blocking the experience of the cosmic energy flow, through objectification and defensiveness. Of course, this is an appealing option because it provides excitement and a sense of meaning in life. Instead of the recognition that would come with standing forth as a True Self, much attention is rewarded for standing out as a False self. On the social and political levels, the False self, with its achievements, obligations, morality, and law, is honored by others, while the True self is discouraged and often punished.

Empathy connects at a superficial level; resonance reminds us of a pre-existing connection at our deepest levels. There is nothing to be gained or lost. There are only relationships to be acknowledged, and the Self to be discovered; these are inextricably bound one to the other.

Notes

1. Webster's Collegiate Dictionary (Springfield, MA: G. and C. Merriam, 1947).
2. W. Reich, *Selected Writings* (New York: Farrar, Straus and Giroux, 1973), 53.

ENERGY

Shiatsu, rolfing, acupuncture, polarity therapy, Reichian body work, acupressure, and various forms of massage all utilize the concept of an underlying energy that can be released. Whether this energy is called ch'i, or prana, or vital force, or simply energy, the assumptions about it are similar. We have noticed that people with an energy model tend to set up a limitation by reifying the energy—that is, viewing the energy as physical stuff, with physical properties. The following assumptions are useful in moving beyond the restrictions of this mechanistic, physicalized concept of energy. They are not necessarily true; rather, they are ways to think about energy in order to introduce new perspectives.

Energy is a verb, not a noun. There is no such thing as energy; there is only *activity* that is described in terms of energy. So, when we speak of "life energy," this term describes activity, not a measurable physical entity. A person does not possess energy "stuff" that is bound up and needs release; rather, the individual expresses more personal potential by active engagement with the world.

Energy concepts help to describe invisible events. The individual is involved in an active, dynamic *process.* In the Chinese articulation, energy is seen as like the wind, which is invisible but has visible effects, such as the waves on top of a pond stirred by a breeze. The concept of energy is merely a useful way of describing the deeper, hidden patterns that underlie the visible effects of the personality.

Energy is relationship in action. Ida Rolf, the inventor of structural integration, once said that the energy of the body exists in the relationship of the body structure to itself. If the structures are bound together, the energy is *fixed;* if the structures have a more fluid relationship, the energy is less fixed and hence more abundant *in its effects.* A variety of different energy conditions are possible at different times in an individual's life; the ancient Chinese concept of the five elements (the "five stages of change") codifies the categories within which the myriad energy states tend to organize. When someone is radiantly alive, we speak of that person as possessing an abundance of *free* life energy; conversely, an individual is said to be *blocked* in expression of energy in the states of illness or depression. Death is an absence of energy, a cessation of the life process. If an individual is radiantly alive, this does not mean that the person has an abundance of some entity; if the person is depressed, it does not mean that some *thing* is lacking—rather, the energy is bound up in fixed patterns. Furthermore, there is no good energy and bad energy; there are merely *different conditions* in which the individual's life process participates. It is not good to have high energy and not bad to have low energy; "high energy" merely describes situations wherein the individual has much freedom of possibility and responsiveness, and "low energy states" involve retraction, and less differentiation of expression.

Energy is a process of change. Life energy is a *process* in a continual flux. There are alternatives of rest and movement, unfolding and infolding, evolution and involution. All that remains constant is the process of change itself; even nonchange is seen as a temporary event in the process of change. This is the "forever flowing constancy" of Taoist philosophy.

The concept of energy can be used to engender a holistic approach. The complaint of many people seeking attention for symptoms is that a mechanistic approach, which sees their symptoms as physically based, tends to ignore other dimensions of their being. Utilizing concepts of energy to express the relationship between the various dimensions of the person can overcome the tendency to reduce the individual to an aggregate of symptoms. Von Bertalanffy puts it this way:

> We may state as a characteristic of modern science that [the] scheme of isolable units acting in one-way causality has proved to be insufficient. Hence, the appearances in all fields of science of notions like wholeness, holistic, organismic, gestalt, etc., which all signify that in the last resort, we must think in terms of systems of elements in mutual interaction.[1]

Thus, energy can be seen to be the process of *integration* that unifies all dimensions of the individual—body, mind, spirit, emotions, and environment—into a whole person. The energy is the relationship that exists between the various dimensions. The concept of energy provides a belief system by which to articulate the correspondence of one dimension with the others.

The energy body matrix may or may not exist. From the viewpoint of traditional Chinese acupuncture theory, there is an energy body that underlies the other dimensions of being, radiating and giving rise to them. This *energy body matrix* is visualized as a circuitry of channels called *meridians*. Much scientific investigation has been devoted to the question of whether these meridians exist. Although the energy theory can explain some effects that have been experienced, no anatomical channels have been found, and no physical energy stuff has been isolated. But it does not really matter whether the energy exists and flows through meridians or not: this is merely a belief system, useful for organizing our perspective on reality. It is neither true nor false; it is merely a system of concepts. One does not have to prove that the energy exists in order to utilize the concept, any more than one has to accept that an actor on a stage is in fact the character represented in order to be moved by what is said. The process of utilizing any new belief system involves the willing suspension of disbelief—ceasing to resist long enough to see how the world looks when one assumes such a perspective.

The energy concept is a practical, useful personality theory. The practical utility of the energy concept is that it provides a framework by which one can view another individual as a whole person, and can consider the life process as it manifests in a number of perspectives. So, when a person sits in front of you, you can imagine this to be an energy event, which is indeed that individual's personality manifestation at a given point in time. Fundamentally, the aim is not to unblock or release energy: it is for an individual to find more possibilities for a rewarding, full life. By appreciating the interrelationships of that person within interpersonal and intrapersonal realms, we can come to the recognition of the presence of the other. Finally, what one can do in interaction with a client or friend is to appreciate the phenomenon of dialogue, where two energies meet. In this meeting, both individuals are challenged to become more present to themselves and each other; what occurs is the unfolding and expression of the potentials of each individual's personality. Such a dialogue occurs on all dimensions—physical, emotional, intellectual, and spiritual. In any body approach, there are these energy meetings at all the levels; thus, when one touches another person physically, there are many other nonphysical interactions. By utilizing nonconstrictive energy concepts, we make it possible to move beyond the limitations of the purely physical.

What is energy? On the one hand, energy is nothing but a series of concepts useful in describing human life. On the other, it is the miracle of life that emerges as one human soul is revealed to another; it underlies the ineffable, mysterious event that occurs at the meeting of Self and other, where both are touched.

Notes
1.   L. Von Bertalanffy, *General Systems Theory* (New York: Macmillan, 1984), 45.

Recommended Reading
Buber, M. *I and Thou*. New York: Charles Scribner's Sons, 1970.
Porkert, M. *The Theoretical Foundations of Chinese Medicine: Systems of Correspondence*. Cambridge: M.I.T. Press, 1974.
Whitehead, A.N. *Science and the Modern World*. New York: Free Press, 1967.
Wilber, K. *The Spectrum of Consciousness*. Wheaton,IL: Quest, 1977.
Wilhelm, R. and Baynes, C. (Trans.). *The I Ching, or Book of Changes*. Princeton: Princeton University Press, 1967.
Wong, B.R. and McKeen, J. Transpersonal Experience Through Body Approaches. In S. Boorstein (Ed.), *Transpersonal Psychotherapy*. Palo Alto: Science and Behaviour Press, 1980.

WESTERN AND EASTERN MEDICINE: COLLISION OR COOPERATION?

A medical model is a product of the culture in which it develops. The basic assumptions of a society, which generally are not questioned, form the foundation of the medicine that is practised within that society. From the very beginning, eastern and western medicine have developed from utterly different assumptions. To clarify the differences between these two medical forms, we need to understand the roots of eastern and western cultures. We will use the term "western medicine" primarily to mean allopathic medicine as practised in the United States and Canada; "eastern medicine" will for the most part refer to traditional Chinese medicine, as this is the eastern form with which the authors are most familiar.

Western thought has culminated in the scientific method. Analysis and logic are the underpinnings of western culture. Western language is one of *separation* and *distinctions*; subject, verb, object. The underlying assumption is one of separateness, each individual acting on a world and being acted on by it. The prototype of this way of thinking is Newtonian mechanical physics, which investigates the laws that govern the behavior of discrete particles in space and time. One assumes a causal order in the universe, where one event in space and time precedes and affects events that follow it.

Eastern thought has developed in a different milieu. From its beginnings, Chinese culture has assumed a *unity* underlying apparent diversity. *Participation* and *intuition* are the mainstays of operation. The language forms do not make distinctions in the same manner as those in the west. For example, the Chinese language is made up of ideograms—pictures that represent reality. There is less emphasis on things separate in space and time, and more emphasis on *process* and *interrelationship*. In addition to causal order, other dimensions of operation are assumed, where events take place in space and time operating with an "acausal connectedness" (synchronicity).

In the past several centuries, some advanced thinkers in the east and the west have moved toward integration of these two ways of thinking. Although the assumptions of the two world views are very different, we now have an opportunity to create an amalgam of them. Specifically in reference to eastern and western medicine, we believe that it is possible to achieve a functional relationship between these two vastly different approaches, by understanding the attributes of each system.

DIFFERENCES IN THE TWO APPROACHES

The western world has largely misunderstood oriental medical perspectives. With the opening of exchange between China and the west, we now have an opportunity to clarify our information and to forge a relationship between two very different perspectives on health, illness, and healing. Traditional western medicine assumes a separation of human beings into *parts*; this dualism extends to a distinction between mind and body, and emotions and spirit. The traditional oriental approach, however, emphasizes the relationship between *interpenetrating* dimensions (body/mind/spirit/emotions/environment); thus, eastern medicine is *holistic* in its view.

Whereas traditional western medicine has grown up within the *scientific analytical* heritage, eastern medicine has from the beginning used a much more *phenomenological* approach. In the west it is important to stand back, observe, and then diagnose and act on the patient as an outside agent. In the eastern approach, the practitioner blends with the patient and comes to appreciate the world through the patient's eyes; the resonance of empathy that comes from this close meeting is analogous to diagnosis, and treatment emerges in the dynamic interplay of the personalities of the practitioner and client.

SPECIFIC ISSUES

One can find merits and shortfalls in both eastern and western approaches to medicine. Western medicine falls short in appreciation of the "world" of the patient. The natural healing approach of eastern medicine is less decisive in its ability to intervene (for example, in emergencies), and can be less effective in acute situations. Whereas the traditional western approach has emphasized treatment of illness, the traditional Chinese approach has stressed health and way of life rather than the disease process itself. Moreover, the underlying theme in western preventive medicine is *blame* for the results of life stances and activities; the eastern approach is more compatible with *consequences* for actions. The western system is a moral one, rooted in causal thinking; the eastern approach is amoral, developed out of associative thinking.

Traditional oriental medicine is interested in curing disease before it manifests. Eastern medicine assumes that disease is a manifestation of blocks in the energy matrix; these blocks can give rise to disease within any of the various dimensions of being (physical/emotional/mental/spiritual/environmental). The aim in Oriental medicine is to understand and reharmonize the life-style pattern of the individual, before the disordered pattern has a chance to get a deep hold and manifest as disease. Oriental medicine is anticipatory and emphasizes life-style.

Traditional western medicine has developed into a magnificent system of cures. Once a disease has manifested, the western approach has elegant and far-reaching ways of dealing with it. The assumption is that diseases are "things," entities, which develop within the mind, *or* the body, *or* the emotions, *or* the spirit. Intervention occurs after the disease has manifested. There is a great difference in Chinese medical science (which is a phenomenological, inductive approach) and western medical science (which is analytic and deductive). Thus, it is difficult for western science, which has investigated "things," to comprehend a science that has studied "dynamisms." The methodologies and assumptions underlying the two approaches are different; however, they are quite complementary when well understood and practised. Whereas western science has largely been quantitative, Chinese science has emphasized qualitative analysis. Western science has set out to be wholly objective; Chinese science includes the subjective experience of the human participant-observer. At this stage in history, Chinese science is incorporating the western scientific approach; western science now has an opportunity to learn much from the rich legacy of traditional Chinese science.

Language is made up of assumptions that construct reality. There is a tendency to believe that what one sees is "true" rather than the product of a way of thinking, a perspective. For example, in the west there is an inclination to think that the only reality is one that can be described in our western terminology. As the language of the west lends itself to a subject-object dichotomy, our "reality" is one of separate objects. In the Chinese culture, a pictorial series of ideographs make up a fluid relational language in which the whole is emphasized. A concept of energy that underlies physical reality is a natural consequence of such a language.

Translations of relational Chinese ideas into reifying western language have often involved misinterpretations of the oriental concepts. Sometimes these concepts are rejected as "antiquated" or simplistic, because they are not appreciated in light of the culture from which they were derived. Many of the oriental theories are very sophisticated, with profound application. An example involves the "five stages of change," a cornerstone theory of eastern medicine that is generally mistranslated as the "five elements" and rejected as outmoded. This theory involves a subtle understanding of change and development of personality (analogous to Piaget's concepts in western psychology[1]). The ideas involved in Chinese medicine have a long history of development; indeed, the concepts are still unfolding in the light of modern research. It is poor logic to dismiss an entire medical system because of the deep historical roots of its conceptual matrix.

Acupuncture has been seen in the west as the main component of oriental medicine, and has been misunderstood as merely a tool for analgesia. Most of acupuncture is not for pain relief; this is a recent and somewhat incidental use of a broad-based medical perspective. Until now, western medicine has tried to incorporate acupuncture into itself as a tool, rather than seeing it as a function of a highly integrated medical system that goes far beyond mere relief of symptoms. Acupuncture is not itself a total system of medicine. Rather, it is an important approach in traditional Chinese medicine (along with moxibustion, herbalism, diet, massage, and life-style counselling). To consider oriental medicine as only acupuncture would be as inappropriate as to say that the prescribing of antibiotics is the entirety of western medicine.

Modern western medicine relies upon technological tools to facilitate diagnosis and treatment; traditional oriental medicine emphasizes the experiential interaction of practitioner and client without the use of elaborate ancillary tools. Because the Chinese approach emphasizes pulse diagnosis and involves little use of machinery and technology, it can be seen as imprecise. However, pulse diagnosis is an exhaustive correlation of numerous qualities and parameters that together provide a deep clinical picture of the individual. As well, detailed history-taking and physical examination are important tools of classical Chinese diagnosis.

Western medicine boasts a long line of medical practitioners who were well versed in life-style counselling and in appreciating the whole patient. Dr. William Osler, the father of Canadian medicine, had much to say about the art of medicine (incidentally, he used acupuncture as part of his medical approach).[2] Western medicine has in recent years been involved in technological development, and the teaching of the art of medicine has been de-emphasized. By appreciating eastern medicine, which stresses the art, western medicine can learn about its own roots.

RECOMMENDATIONS

One could say the western approach is too hard and distancing; on the other hand, one could criticize eastern perspectives as too soft and lacking in objectivity. We propose that a mature medical perspective involves a synthesis of these two approaches. A practitioner should be able to move fluidly from one point of view to the other. In a sense, it should be possible to put on eastern medical glasses that permit a subjective, close-up view of the patient's condition. It should then be possible to adopt the more objective viewpoint, analyzing and acting from a distance. Optimal learning would arise out of a framework of thesis-antithesis-synthesis.

Life-style counselling is sometimes misinterpreted by western thinkers as a system of blame. There is considerable difference between "I am responsible for my illness process" (I am the one who is involved in this process) and "I am to blame for my illness" (I caused my illness). The term "preventive medicine" implies a moralistic perspective, according to which disease is a bad thing to be rooted out. From a meta-perspective, illness and health are seen in dynamic interplay, with a holistic appreciation of the causes and consequences of illnesses and health. An integrated practitioner would not harangue patients about their life-style, but would instead educate about the *consequences* of life-style choices.

The concept of disease should be deeply understood. From the perspective of clinical philosophy, disease is merely one consequence of a nonvital life pattern; it is neither good or bad, but simply a result of life-energy patterning.[3] We believe that a practitioner should be able to recognize the subtle signs of the presence or absence of life and wellness. As well, one can be equally versed in traditional western and eastern approaches to the diagnosis and treatment of illness conditions, and can take a synthetic approach to counselling for life and wellness enhancement.

It is worth stating that practitioners should study their own personal health/illness and vitalizing/constraining orientations. A limitation of the western approach is that physicians readily assume they are studying others. However, they can learn much from their own life, including their health and illness experiences. An integrated practitioner *resonates* with others through the medium of his/her own life matrix while maintaining a functional level of objectivity.

Traditional Chinese medicine is not an enemy of western medical science; neither is it a quaint, outmoded approach to be discarded. Each system of thought has much to learn from the other. It would be a tragic shortcoming to lose the potential benefits of mutual understanding owing to a myopic, prejudiced attitude. We propose that the most constructive vantage point is to see Chinese science (with acupuncture being a case in point) as a system of thought with its own parameters, modes of operation, and consequences, and to see western science as a different system of thought. If one were to achieve this eminently mature intellectual perspective, it would be possible to construct a meta-science that would include understanding from both seemingly contradictory systems. This does call for a broad vision; it involves seeing the thought structures through the lens of general systems theory and from an evolutionary rather than a fixed perspective. If, after all, what we are concerned with is the health and well-being of humanity, then we are called upon to overcome our limited viewpoints and to achieve the most beneficial perspective for the sake of the individuals seeking medical attention, and for the advancement of science.

Notes

1. J. Piaget, *The Principles of Genetic Epistemology*. translated by Wolfe Mays (New York: Basic Books, 1972).
2. W. Osler, *Aequanimitas* (New York: McGraw-Hill, 1906).
3. P. Koestenbaum, *The New Image of the Person: The Theory and Practice of Clinical Philosophy* (Westport, CT: Greenwood Press, 1978), 463-65.

Recommended Reading

Sobel, D. (Ed.). *Ways of Health: Holistic Approaches to Ancient and Contemporary Medicine*. New York: Harcourt Brace Jovanovich, 1979.

Kaptchuk, T. *The Web That Has No Weaver: Understanding Chinese Medicine*. New York: Congdon and Weed, 1983.

Individual Responsibility in Illness and Health

In earliest times it seemed that a person's well-being was related to survival, through the avoidance of physical threats and hostile environments. As nature became more controllable, there arose superstitious beliefs in powerful spirits and gods that could do harm to individuals, sometimes just for sport. In recent centuries, the scientific philosophy gave rise to the discovery of a great number of causative agents (bacterial, viral, and chemical) that could negatively affect a person's well-being.

The net effect of a scientific approach to health is to cast humankind into an adversarial role in relationship to the environment. Healthy survival then depends upon how well the environment is controlled. For example, if we are not careful to shield ourselves from the possibility of a viral attack, we will likely succumb to a cold; we become "victims" to some invading forces that "lack respect" for our integrity and well-being. Belief in such forces would cause us to avoid all sources of possible contamination (people) as well as set off a drive to clean up the environment, way beyond any reasonable standard. Basically, such an attitude derives from a paranoid position that requires vigilance and care in order to avoid ill health. We fortify our defenses to protect us from these ever-present noxious invaders; in so doing, we also produce an increasing separation between ourselves and our environments.

What many people do not recognize is that many of these "enemies" are omnipresent, living comfortably or in harmony nearby, or perhaps even somewhere within our bodies. A simple example is the cold virus, which probably lives in most of our throats most of the time. When, then, do we come down with a cold? We commonly believe that the virus has been waiting for the opportunity to "invade" our bodies, perhaps when we get overly tired or when we eat the wrong things. For a moment, consider the possibility that sometimes a cold can be useful, that the helplessness it produces might serve us. Certainly, as children we learn that helplessness provides us with many secondary benefits—we get attention; we get excused from chores, school, or work; and perhaps we even receive special foods. Is it possible that when we grow older, we are not above reaping the benefits of a cold—perhaps a rationalization for a much-needed rest which we otherwise would feel too guilty to take? Certainly, in the climate of our current times, the helpless receive much more attention and assistance than do the competent.

The idea that we are responsible for our own illness patterns may explain some hitherto inexplicable behavior—why the obese continue to overeat, or alcoholics continue to drink even though it is ruining their lives, or people with heart disease or emphysema continue to smoke. Although they would like to believe that they are helpless victims of their addictions, it is apparent that they benefit in some way from their symptoms. Perhaps the obese person is attempting to pad the body as a means of avoiding intimacy; perhaps the alcoholic is afraid to face the possibility of failure, so drinks so that nobody will expect much; perhaps the smoker is keeping feelings under control because to express real feelings (such as anger or passion) may drive others away. Whatever the behavior, the body cooperates with symptoms of an illness process that serves the person's particular needs, be they emotional or spiritual. Thus, whenever a person has symptoms, or a diagnosed illness, there is an underlying meaning of these symptoms to be discovered. The body will speak what the mouth cannot, or *will* not!

The ancient Chinese conceived of the essence of life as an entity called "ch'i" energy. Their hypothesis was that this life-force energy comes into the being at the time of conception, exists in the individual throughout his or her lifetime, and departs at death. During the person's life, the ch'i energy continually flows through meridian pathways; the pattern created by this flow constitutes the energy body matrix, which is seen as the essence of the organism. This pattern and its radiation underlie all the dimensions of a person—spiritual, emotional, physical, and intellectual. In the view of the ancients, if the energy flow in the matrix is balanced and harmonious, the organism functions freely, without illness. To the extent that blocks or fixations arise within the energy body, there will be a disruption in the harmony and balance at the level of essence, creating difficulty within the various dimensions of the person. Illness is seen as resulting from blockages within the essence pattern; these blockages cause the energy to deviate from the healthy state into illness patterns that are manifested intellectually, physically, emotionally, and spiritually. Only in the unblocked healthy state can the human organism develop fully and grow creatively; the illness blocks impede the process of individuation.

The person who has an illness on any of the dimensions of being is creating and sustaining blocks to the vital energy flow; hence, each individual is *responsible* (but *not* to blame) for illness. The blocks may be generated and maintained by subconscious processes; nevertheless, at some level, the individual maintains the illness pattern.

EMOTIONAL BLOCKS

By withholding the expression of emotions, a person produces blocks in the energy body matrix, creating illness patterns in the essence energy. The mechanisms to inhibit emotional expression include *withdrawal*, *repression*, and *denial*. By becoming aware of the nature of these mechanisms, one can overcome them and learn to express emotions instead of repressing them. The more the individual can let emotions flow, the more the life energy can run freely and the more that healing and awareness can grow within the Self. Often the individual encounters a great deal of fear overlaying the blocked emotions. By refusing to flee from the fear, the person can allow the emotions to emerge; beneath fears lies a vast amount of experience from which learning and growth can occur.

PHYSICAL BLOCKS

Illness is also created and sustained on the physical level. Lack of exercise engenders sluggishness and dis-ease. Certain exercises done in an ambitious, goal-oriented way tend to tighten the physical being into a particular pattern, producing restriction and lack of flow. The physical limitations correspond to a rigidly patterned energy body matrix. Goal-oriented athletics often produces blocks. Expressive exercise, such as free-form t'ai chi and creative dance, are probably better for fluid energy flow than are tightly disciplined activities. In fact, any exercise done creatively to express the Self will help to open up the organism; any activity that is goal directed will produce contraction. And yet if one is a goal-oriented person, one cannot simply deny one's tendency; one can learn to become more fluid, even in the midst of striving.

The maintenance of the open healthy state is also determined by what one ingests. A well-balanced diet engenders healthy functioning and growth, whereas an inadequate diet fails to provide the necessary nourishment. The use of alcohol, nicotine, and other drugs can also create blocks, limiting the natural expression of the Self.

SPIRITUAL BLOCKS

Illness can manifest at the spiritual level; as well, blocks at the spiritual dimension can create illness. Victor Frankl said that "man's search for meaning is a primary force in his life."[1] In creativity, man expresses meaning beyond the Self. Frankl quotes Nietzsche: "He who has a *why* to live for can bear almost any *how*."[2] When this sense of meaning is lost, illness patterns may substitute for it. Spiritual death comes with the loss of personal creative meaning. To find personal meaning in life and to channel energy into creative activity aids the spiritual rebirth that generates health, well-being, and growth.

Overly disciplined spiritual activity can also result in blocks to free expression. Excessive involvement in yoga, meditation, special diets, and so on can limit the individual rather than expand awareness. Inherent in excessive discipline is spiritual ambition; literally, the individual wants to get somewhere spiritually. In this ambition and the patterned behavior that results, a tightening occurs in the energy matrix, producing a contraction in the person. In a paradoxical way, the ambition to become spiritually expanded results in a contracted state. The first step in overcoming this contraction is awareness that excessive spiritual discipline can induce it; this awareness may facilitate greater expansion and freer self-expression.

INTELLECTUAL BLOCKS

Intellectual openness and fluidity sustain health and growth. Fixed intellectual patterns restrict the being; illness can result from such limitation. The intellect performs the symbolization of life experiences; one of its main functions is communication. Investment in specific concepts to the exclusion of others constitutes a rigidification into a judgmental attitude. Such an attitude creates much of the contraction in the energy state that underlies many illnesses. Acknowledging rigidity and working toward more intellectual fluidity and openness promotes healing and growth. With the awareness that one's attitude contributes to the creation and maintenance of illness, one can use symptoms as biofeedback, to alert one to the possibility of attitudinal rigidity. By this process of awareness, one can deeply affect the condition of the energy state.

Each of us creates our own life situation and is responsible for our state of health or disease. Wherever illness is present—spiritual, emotional, physical, intellectual, or environmental—the individual is responsible for the creation and maintenance of the patterns that underlie the illness. Once again, *this responsibility is not blame*; it merely acknowledges the individual's participation. By accepting responsibility for sickness and health, one can move through and beyond illness patterns, into states of health and openness. In the healthy open state, the person can grow and mature, to reach the full depth and expanse of self-expression and individuation.

Disease is nothing but life under altered conditions.[3]

—Virchow

Notes
1. V.E. Frankl, *Man's Search For Meaning* (New York: Simon and Schuster, 1962), 97.
2. Ibid., p. 76.
3. Rudolf Virchow quoted in Karl Menninger, Martin Mayman and Paul Pruyser, *The Vital Balance* (New York: Viking Press, 1963), 41.

Recommended Reading
Connelly, D. *Traditional Acupuncture: The Law of the Five Elements.* Columbia: Center for Traditional Acupuncture, 1979.

THE HELPING RELATIONSHIP

Since the turn of the twentieth century, the helping professions (including medicine, psychology, and the other social sciences) have been affected by a series of social events that can be divided into three broad periods: (1) the mechanistic era, (2) the communications era, and (3) the structuralist era. These eras have had a marked influence on the values and practices in the helping fields.

THE MECHANISTIC ERA

Most of the advances of the early twentieth century came about because of an adherence to scientific thought and discipline; the human organism was seen as a miracle of mechanical perfection whose working parts could be isolated, studied, fixed, and even replaced when damaged or lost. This *medical model*, mechanistic in nature, greatly influenced Freud and his professional descendants, so that modern psychology contained within it a number of attitudes sometimes described as "psychohydraulics." In general medicine, most attention was given to the efficient working of the various parts rather than to the whole person. Contained within this model was a belief in *authority*, which was invested in the top few who, it was believed, knew what was right or good for the majority. This hierarchical attitude dominated the physician-patient relationship, spawning within patients a sense of helplessness about themselves while fostering a feeling of awe and dependence upon the physician-healer.

From the beginning of this century, psychiatry, though less scientific in nature, developed these same characteristics because of its alliance with the medical, mechanistic model. Attention was given to those with poor working parts or whose functioning and performance became inefficient or somehow deviant from the norm.

THE COMMUNICATIONS ERA

Toward the end of the Second World War there developed a broad new understanding of communications, ushered in by rapid changes in electronic technology, much of which had been developed for the purposes of war. The onset of the communications era was rapid and dramatic, reaching its peak in the sixties when its offspring were old enough to exert power and influence over the direction of society's systems. Social and political disorder were some of the negative aspects of this revolution; in the behavioral sciences there developed a great interest in means of enhancing communication between people, giving rise to theories of social psychology and communications schools of thought. This was the generation of immediate gratification, the "here and now" interest in the present, the rapid identification with groups (minority, majority, special interest, and so on) and the valuing of change, often merely for the sake of change itself. The prevailing fear of the individual was *fear of isolation*; people had to "belong."

In this atmosphere of communication, humanistic psychology rose to the fore, championed by growth centers such as Esalen in California and popularized by the media. Being dissatisfied with traditional psychotherapy, which appeared to be lengthy, time consuming, of limited availability to the public, and apparently relatively unsuccessful, humanistic practitioners developed a wide spectrum of techniques, some new, many ancient. Thus, a whole new array of techniques and vocabulary was developed outside the auspices of traditional psychology and medicine, such as gestalt therapy, rolfing, encounter groups, T-groups, psychodrama, art and drama therapy, dance and movement therapy, meditation, Reichian breathing, primal therapy, and transactional analysis. Many of these techniques are now being assimilated into institutional programs and educational centers. However, professional bodies representing traditional schools of thought and practice (such as universities, and medical and psychological organizations) were often somewhat resistant to what was derisively described as the popular activity of the new narcissistic breed.

THE STRUCTURALIST ERA

In the past two decades, the sociocultural landscape has again undergone a major shift. Led by environmentalists who had become aware of the self-destructive trend of the human animal (which was also breeding destruction of other species and the environment), a whole new wave of awareness swept the western world. A natural philosophy of *interdependence* began to be voiced by sociologists and anthropologists who saw an order in the universe based upon *interrelated systems*. What became important to health practitioners of this philosophy were the patterns of individual behavior (life-style), which needed to be clarified so that each individual could have more awareness of this *responsibility* in life itself. Consequences of behavior, freedom of choice with sensitivity to others, and valuing of individuality and idiosyncrasies became more important than communication. The great individual fear became *fear of loss of Self*, of identity, of uniqueness. This structuralist philosophy is gradually creeping into all walks of life. As with communications techniques, however, the traditional helping professions have shown little interest (other than active resistance) in these changes. Because of the important implications they have for the helping professions, politically as well as therapeutically, these new perspectives are dangerous to ignore.

METHODS OF HELP

To the traditionalist, illness is a mechanical malfunctioning requiring mechanical alteration (drugs, diet, or surgery) to correct it. From this mechanistic view, illness is accidental, a result of helplessness or aging, a failure of will, or a victimization by external circumstances. From the perspective of the communications approach, illness represents a pattern of communication. People presenting with symptoms are attempting to "say" something about their experience of the world that they are unable to express in any other way. Thus, there is contained within any illness, psychological or physical, a story from that person's life.

Often clients are unaware of the messages they are trying to convey through their illnesses; indeed, it is generally this lack of understanding of what is trying to be communicated that results in the production of symptoms. Illness exists in face of a *failure to communicate* in any other way. A dramatic example of this is blindness in conversion hysteria, wherein the person expresses an unwillingness to see or face something. A more mundane example is the angry eruptions in psoriasis, which manifest because of a person's inability to express anger more directly. Implicit in this concept is the notion that if people could find others ways to communicate, they would not have to be sick. People who are manifesting illness often feel isolated, alone, and not understood; and they are not understanding themselves.

A practitioner functioning in the communications mode will be attentive not just to the *content* of the client's story, but also to the *quality* of the presentation, alert for clues that help to fill in the full meanings that the person is trying to convey, often unconsciously. The practitioner acts as a good listener, attempting to understand the client's situation and to help the client to come to that understanding. When this is effective the client feels understood, and hence no longer feels isolated. A therapeutic session in this mode functions in much the same way as does the confessional; the person overcomes the barriers that create isolation by contacting another human being, in this case the practitioner. The failure to communicate is overcome, and the illness is then not necessary.

The difficulty with the communication approach is that, although the symptoms are often alleviated, lasting change often does not occur. The client may feel understood and less isolated in contact with the listening physician, yet after the appointment returns to the same life-style, and continues to live in the way that created the illness pattern in the first place (for example, alcoholism). We believe that no lasting change can occur without individuals becoming aware of the *contextual patterns* in which they live.

In the structuralist approach, clients are seen to be full, active agents in their own lives. When there is illness, individuals are not victims of outside forces; rather, they participate in the world in a way that creates illness. Illness persists because of the lack of awareness of the patterns that produce it. When clients become aware of these patterns, they alter or avoid them. This *responsibility* for the Self, including the illness patterns, is different from blame. A person is responsible for having a cold, or a broken arm, insofar as (s)he is the one experiencing this phenomenon; thus, the individual participates in the illness process. However, the person with the illness is *not* to blame; no one is. This is not a moral situation. Rather, from the structuralist viewpoint, all that is significant is the awareness of *process*, and coming to appreciate one's relationship to one's process. With adequate awareness, the relationship to the illness process can change.

Practitioners functioning in the structuralist framework adopt a phenomenological approach. The aim is, as fully as possible, to come to see and appreciate the world through the client's eyes. These practitioners will not try to manipulate their clients' lives from arm's length (mechanistic approach) or passively listen and understand (communication mode); instead, they become *involved* in their clients' experiences, mutually sharing thoughts, interpretations, and feelings as a way of facilitating clients' awareness of themselves in relationship to their practitioners, and ultimately to their families, society, and the entire world.

Recommended Reading
Levenson, E.A. *The Fallacy of Understanding*. New York: Basic Books, 1972.

THERAPY AND EDUCATION

When a person faces a particular problem in life, the question arises as to what is needed: therapy or education? Webster defines "therapy" as "the treatment of disability or disease, as by some remedial or curative process";[1] the word itself is derived from the Greek word "therapeia," which refers to service rendered to the *sick*. Therapy assumes that problems result from illness, that human experience would be free and easy were it not for some breakdown in the body or mind of the person, or some weakness in the body or mind that made it vulnerable to invasion or ill effects from without. The person is a somewhat helpless agent in face of the forces of trauma, bacteria, other people, institutions, and social systems. In this framework, the underlying assumptions are mechanistic and accepting of a victim philosophy.

Scientific principles dominate western thought and increasingly dominate the thought of the rest of the globe. In the usual interpretation, science assumes that the universe and all the people in it are like well-oiled machines, made up of interacting parts that must function in an orderly, predictable, and comprehensible fashion in order to ensure survival. In this paradigm, something or somebody is malfunctioning when a part of the whole no longer performs its customary duties, interfering with the predictable and assigned function of the total organism. If a part fails, the machine declines in efficiency or stops altogether; that broken or "sick" part must be found and repaired, or replaced. The attitude is the same, whether the defective item be an automobile, washing machine, alcoholic, criminal, cancer patient, or schizophrenic.

In the mechanistic model, the machine or (human) organism must be well cared for in order to ensure proper functioning. The breaking-in period of a new automobile ensures later good functioning; this is not much different than the prevailing cautions about child raising. When in later life a person "breaks down," the main question seems to be the nature of the person's early childhood, the "breaking-in" period; what went wrong *then*? Something *wrong* was done to these children at some time in their life. Here we see a subtle but definite attitude of victimhood in which blame can be ascribed to parents, priests, teachers, germs, institutions, societies or anybody that is thought to have power. The victims of such experiences are deemed to be in need of therapy, to return them to happy and efficient functioning, in which they are capable of maintaining their places and functions in the orderly scheme of society.

In such therapy, the recipient (client) assumes a position of relative helplessness. The therapist knows best, and in many instances is credited not only with superior knowledge but also with magical powers. Client and therapist are joined in the task of uncovering the perpetrator(s) of the "illness" causing malfunctioning. Once the villain is determined (insight), proper action depends on the culture and the times. Currently, it is fashionable to finger the culprits and publicly humiliate them, as has repeatedly been done throughout history. The French did it with the guillotine during their revolution, the Chinese did it during their Cultural Revolution; witches were treated this way in Europe, as were suspected communists in the U.S. Christians have had it both ways, originally being persecuted by the Romans, only to turn around and do the same to others later (as they savagely did during the Crusades, and in more civilized fashion recently as the Moral Majority, in their campaigns against anything with which they disagree); in addition, Christians have done the same to themselves (as evidenced in the evangelistic movement's persecutions of their own ministers). Now, the race is on to point the finger at sex abusers, perpetrators of family violence, sexual harassers, and all violators of power in the workplace. Certainly, it seems highly desirable to identify and to change these situations. But can it not be done without emphasizing the helplessness of the so-called victim?

As with therapy, many of society's "cures" for unhealthy behavior and situations reinforce the helplessness of the victim. Our welfare assistance programs, our soup kitchens, and many of our government bureaucracies contribute to this helplessness. Although such programs are established to fill real needs, the tendency of people is to begin to expect such aid as a right, an entitlement that, if used when not really needed, serves to promote a greater sense of helplessness. In Canada, our once nearly ideal health services system is in danger of erosion by such an attitude among its users. Our legal system is becoming a large industry of people demanding redress for victimization by others. Our unions, our professional organizations, and our special-interest groups are all gaining more control over our lives, in their constant efforts to ensure that our individual interests are being preserved. As they become more powerful, we become more helpless, more dependent on them, more ready to complain, to whine, to demand. Our sense of personal responsibility, the feeling of being in charge of our own lives, of being the directors of our own affairs, is gradually slipping from our hands.

Working with people over a combined sixty years of practice and teaching has led us to believe that those who need the most help, physically or emotionally, are those who have given in to the seduction of believing that they are the victims of external circumstances. Because of their belief that they are helpless agents in the scheme of their own lives, they have an inherent trust in therapy. Somebody out there did them wrong; somebody out there knows how to set it right. In this way of thinking, the therapist knows best. And yet, therapy as it is practised is based on very inexact

approaches that have rarely been able to meet even the most basic requirements of the scientific method, while making claims of understanding and
knowing. This is not to say that many people have not been helped by
therapy; but we should not forget that equal numbers have been helped by
healers of all persuasions, many of whom would be offended to be considered as falling within a scientific framework.

Consider for a moment the suggestions made by the proponents of a
structuralist philosophy: that human beings are more than the sum total of
their parts; that the whole is present in all of the parts; that all behavior is an
expression of the Self and the universe, and so is never abnormal but is
merely *idiosyncratic* (unique). At all levels of being, the Self is always expressing its own idiosyncratic patterns that can be seen and interpreted in
the body, the spirit, the mind, the emotions, and the environment. Any
holding or blocking of energy at any of these levels produces a resistance or
block at all of these levels. Similarly, each individual and all things on earth
express the energy pattern of the earth, which along with all the other
structures of the universe expresses the energy pattern of the total unity. The
various levels are actually a continuum, from the central core of all things to
the superficial expression of each person; this point can be better understood
by artificially dividing the continuum into a "deep" (universal) structure,
which humans share with all things, "sociocultural" (human) structures,
which include familial, national, and cultural patterns, and "idiosyncratic"
("superficial") structures, which are unique to the individual.

Most education at home and school will teach the values and methods of
the sociocultural structures, tending to ignore or devalue the deep or idiosyncratic structures. In this way, walls are constructed and the False self is
developed as an Ideal self. The abandonment of the Authentic Self gives rise
to self-hatred (as discussed above, in "The Ideal Self"). This kind of educational model tends to view the individual as a clean slate, upon which the
educational system will write what is important for that person's survival in
society. An alternative structuralist or holistic view assumes the individual
to have *pre-existing patterns* at all levels of being. In this holistic model,
education provides the stimulus to *awaken inherent potentials* within individuals, helping each person to discover these personal truths within the
Self; such is the nature of "heuristic education," where rote learning is
replaced by situations in which people can discover for themselves. To
summarize the holistic approach, the Self is complete within itself, initially
as potential that requires the stimulation of interpersonal relationships to
grow to fruition. To educators, the challenge is to create situations in which
the Self is able to discover its own possibilities.

Notes
1. *The Living Webster* (Chicago: English Language Institute of America,
   1971).

Allergies and Phobias: Keeping the World at Bay

TWO STORIES

To a casual observer Jane's life is highly successful. She is attractive, well educated, and has a good, well-paying job. But her outward appearance of success masks an inner turmoil that runs deep and disrupts the entire fabric of her life. Jane has been going from doctor to doctor for the past several years, trying to find someone who can explain the extreme, yet vague, symptoms that she experiences. And although many professionals have provided treatments, suggestions, and attention, she still suffers from myriad complaints with little relief. She is puzzled, frustrated, and frightened by what seems to be happening to her. Her inner life is a private hell. Whereas she used to have extraordinary vitality, she has been having increasing difficulty getting through her workdays. She sleeps a fitful thirteen-hour night; she feels tired all the time and does not have enough energy for her other interests or for keeping up with friends. Her friends are beginning to stop calling; more and more, she is by herself at home in bed. Her life dreams are fading as she struggles to get through just one more day. She has been told that her headaches, listlessness, and nasal symptoms add up to an allergy syndrome. She feels a little better on a special allergic diet that has been prescribed, yet she is beginning to fear that she is never going to get well or regain her previous happy, carefree life.

Audrey, who has been experiencing similar fatigue symptoms in a city far away from Jane, seems to be in a different situation. Because of her intense fears of leaving her home, she has been told that she is "agoraphobic." She scarcely ever leaves her apartment; family and friends must come to visit her. Although she conducts her successful business from her home, she is coming to recognize that her life is closing in on her, yet the thought of going out for an evening is so fearful to her that she simply refuses to date. The extreme anxiety she has been feeling for the past several years has been profoundly reduced by her limiting her activities and by the large doses of tranquilizers and antidepressants that she takes daily; yet, with her diminished anxiety, she feels dulled. This attractive young woman is becoming more and more socially paralyzed as her condition takes deeper hold.

THE SCOPE OF THE PROBLEM

There are many more people living similarly restricted lives. A growing number of young people are suffering from apparently different syndromes that have remarkably common underlying themes. Sometimes the diagnosis is "phobia"; at other times the label is "allergy" or, lately, the popular "total allergy syndrome." Yet there are unmistakable common threads that run through the different stories. As we came to know a number of these people over many years, we recognized that all of them are dealing with fundamental issues of *boundary distinction*.

BOUNDARIES

Physiology of Boundaries (The Immune System)

The immunological system is a biological complex that functions to protect the integrity of the physical organism; with its various antibodies, it is like an army that defends from outside invasion. In a sense, the immune system functions to maintain the boundary of the physical being, distinguishing and keeping out what is "not me" and holding in place what is "me." When a person's immune system malfunctions, disease states ensue. For example, allergy involves a hyperreactivity to certain outside conditions (for example, hay fever, drug hypersensitivity, food allergies); the defense is excessive. When the immune system is underactive, as in extremely debilitated states or in illnesses such as AIDS, the person is physically vulnerable to assault from what might ordinarily be harmless circumstances. For example, a person with a lowered immune defense system is more susceptible to infections and is less able to fight them effectively; the physical defenses are down.

Boundaries and Ego Psychology: The Process of Separation/Individuation

In ego psychology terms, the infant "hatches" from the mother-infant "symbiotic dual unity" during the process of ego development. The developmental project of each young child is to become a separate human being by developing a sense of Self that is distinct from the mother (and by extension, distinct from the environment). This project is well under way by two years of age, when the child is first learning to move away from the parent while still craving the protective milieu of parental love and acceptance. The child is in a process of separation (learning to be psychologically and physically separate from the mother) and individuation (developing a unique sense of Self in an individual life experience).

For many children, this process is not smooth; the child either hastily and prematurely splits from the parent instead of developing a separation, or does not separate, remaining symbiotically and dependently bound to the psyche of the parent. In a sense, the child either develops brittle and artificial boundary distinctions (walls) or remains somewhat fused with the parent. The former is analogous to hyperactivity of the immune system; the latter is analogous to inadequate immunity to the outside world. In later relationships, this early defensive pattern of splitting without relating, or fusing without distinction, is likely to be reproduced.

Boundaries in the Chinese Medicine Perspective (The Earth Element)

In the framework of traditional Chinese medicine, the issues of the earth are those of incarnation. In other words, the human body is the medium through which the other dimensions of being are expressed and made manifest. The definition of the individual takes shape and form through the mediation of the earth energies. The earth issues have to do with relationships, the physical being, separation/union, the mother/child interaction, and nurturing. Individuals with difficulties in the earth aspects of the energy body matrix will exhibit symptoms in the body, in relationships, and in definition of the Self.

DISCUSSION OF THE CASES PRESENTED

In the lives of the individuals cited above, and the countless others like them, the dominant theme seems to be a problem with boundary distinctions. The individuals are highly intelligent and generally unusually creative people. Hence, they are unwilling to follow a "standard" life path. However, these people are generally very frightened of the passions that surge through them; they fear their erotic impulses, are anxious about their high level of energy, and are afraid of the unusual thoughts that pass through their minds. These creative individuals are unwilling to live a commonplace existence; yet they are cast into an existential maelstrom of anxiety and uncertainty without sufficiently developed boundaries that would help them to determine where they belong and what they wish to do in the universe. They resist succumbing to the safety of the standard cultural patterns (get a job, get married, and raise children); yet they are reluctant to risk a full-blown creative life. They are caught in the hinterland between the commonplace and the unique. They wall themselves off from the regular world with an illness process; in a sense, they become "allergic" to the commonplace, or develop "phobias" that protect them from conventionality.

However, deep down there is a feeling of despair as they do not fully engage with their life; this is supplanted by symptom complexes. The bulk of their creative energy is devoted to producing an illness metaphor in which they can justifiably live. Instead of devoting themselves to artful living, they become increasingly enslaved by the illness system that they create and maintain. In a way, their illness provides social justification for their unusualness, without the risks of full-blown creativity. The uncertainty of the creative impulse is reduced to the predictability of an illness condition ("I couldn't possibly go there. I can't handle that.")

These people are generally under forty, intelligent and attractive beyond the usual. All of them experience varying degrees of anxiety, fatigue, lessened energy, disturbance of sleep patterns (for example, sleeping up to thirteen or fourteen hours per day without being refreshed), bodily tensions, and symptoms related to eyes, ears, nose, and throat. They are increasingly socially isolated. Although this is often rationalized ("I'm allergic, so I can't go there . . . eat that . . . do this"; "I simply have to get twelve hours of sleep"; "I'm afraid to go out at night—it's a phobia"), there is an underlying *terror of intimacy*. Their relationships are dependent; they will not risk the uncertainty that accompanies the vulnerable exposure of the Self in intimacy and interdependency.

In summary, they have been afraid to face the passion and the creativity that course through them. They generally are afraid of vulnerability and have a *high need for control*. They feel victimized by life, and adopt a stance in which "life does it to me." They tend to recognize that those who follow cultural convention are enslaved and dead. However, they themselves become trapped in their victim stance, which maintains them in the cage of the illnesses they have created.

In the words of one such person:

> I created total allergy sydrome. I experience a great fear in becoming vulnerable and have throughout my life often denied intimacy because of that fear.

> I also experience life very intensely: my emotional range consisted of jagged peaks of joy, even ecstasy, and very deep sadness and pain. The instability that I experienced from this caused much despair in my life, and I sought ways of becoming stable.

> I see total allergy syndrome as an extension of this disconnectedness from my essential self and as a reaction to the denial of my natural life.

> I am terrified of being who I am. I see myself as a little boy overawed by life and fearful of the pain and sadness that I find in life.

Another young person relates:

> My illness is the result of a lack of self-expression.

Another:

> Basically, I am finding that there is something emotional or psychological [that is, ingrained attitudes, behaviors, and suppressed feelings, needs, and desires] behind every physical allergic reaction. Awareness of the underlying factors improves the symptoms and allows me to take charge and control them much of the time.

And another:

> The challenges in my life were masked in attacking the same mundane exercises day in and day out year after year after year.

> I created the fears and these fears help me to survive situations I otherwise wouldn't look at.

> I haven't the means to know what would constitute "value" [in my life] . . . I now know that I have to find my own definition of worth and make a strong and fully conscious decision to live it.

> This place of desolation is a large part of my pattern; it comes up over and over again starting very early in my childhood memories.

> What I've realized here is that my stubborn resistance to my own mortality only serves to further fuel my feelings of fear and anxiety. I also feel that I isolate myself from others at these times and become very lonely.

THE WAY OUT

We have worked with numerous people over the past twenty years who have made significant improvement in these conditions. They have struggled to *take more responsibility* for themselves and their life circumstances (including their symptoms). As they came to see that anxiety is just the life energy coursing through them, they learned to embrace increasing amounts of anxiety. As their tolerance for anxiety increased, they were able to face one of their largest fears: of being close to another human being. As they took increasing responsibility for their process, they began to understand the secret codes of the illness metaphor; they came to see the symptoms as messages from their inner being, calling for reunion with themselves. In a way, the illness, which previously was an enemy, became a friend. At bottom, they were afraid of nonexistence. They were afraid to stand on their own in the face of another person. They were either isolated, or refrained from intimate contact by maintaining dependent relationships.

The following words speak for themselves:

> I've learned that anxiety can be energy running through me.

> I no longer fit into a mold of what I think I should be. I just *am*, marching to a different beat.

> Everything I hold or lock in makes me sick. I need and want to be around people I can let go with.

I believe that I am well, whole, integrating ... that I have learned and know all I need to be well and express myself in the world. What I need and want to do now is develop the self-love and confidence to trust it and do it.

I see my allergies and symptoms as friends/guides to keep me in tune with myself and on my path of health and growth. It is an ongoing process. This is a beginning, not an end.

I also realize that I must surrender myself to the pain, to the sadness, in order to experience the joy and intimacy that life will provide.

I seek now the courage within myself to surrender and to live.

The courage that we have witnessed in people facing these difficult issues has been inspirational. Life springs forth in its majesty in the growth of human personality. The illness process recedes, and creativity begins to flourish.

CREATION-CENTERED SPIRITUALITY

Regardless of their particular problems and their motive for embarking on a voyage of self-discovery, personal growth, or self-healing, most people will wrestle with issues of spirituality and meaning. From the holistic point of view, it could not be otherwise, as blocks or impediments to growth and energy movement always occur simultaneously at all levels of being. Although a person's awareness and focus may be on one of these levels, any movement or changes will find expression on all of the levels. Shifts in body, emotions, or mental attitudes will have spiritual implications, and vice versa.

The term "spirituality" refers to the level of being that addresses the issues of *meaning* in face of the emptiness and void. Too often, spirituality is confused with religion, which is a codification of spirituality. Religion is a sort of map of meaning that is used by institutions and governing authorities to provide a group of people with a morality—rules of behavior and thought aimed at a common goal.

Commonly, people suffered from church experiences in childhood, so they resist any exploration in the direction of spirituality; they confuse religiosity with spirituality. They often believe that along with spirituality will come morality, control, and limitation of their behavior, guilt, recrimination, self-denial, and ultimately self-denigration. Such fears are based in experience of the commonly held belief and teachings of the neo-Platonist redemption-based spirituality.[1] This conservative view, which dominates most traditional western religions, assumes a higher power (God) existing outside the Self. Hence power, control, and morality are issues to be discovered outside of the Self, dictated by some wiser, stronger, and more invulnerable being. The authority for correct behavior exists with that being (read "God") or the agents of that being (read "church"). In their struggle toward autonomy and personal growth, most people must reclaim the strength and personal power that they lost via their upbringing and social training. The authorities that they usually reject include parents, education, and religion, when those have exerted a dominating influence. They could become locked in a power struggle, which tends to prevent rather than aid their growth.

There exists another possible view of spirituality, in which the authority for the Self remains within the individual. Such is the nature of creation-centered spirituality, in which the individual is seen as a part of, and reflective of, the totality of existence (read "God"). As proposed by the philosophy of structuralism, each person is already whole, although the wholeness is usually being expressed in a lower state of resolution. There is nothing to be rid of, or added to, or punished for; there is only more self-awareness and self-responsibility to be experienced. The Self is not striving toward perfection; it is already whole. We are attempting both to know and to accept ourselves more, in order to better reveal to ourselves and to others what already exists within. Ours is a process of revelation and unfolding wholeness, rather than a striving toward a perfection set before us by authorities greater than ourselves. We are forever in a process of creating the expression of ourselves rather than attempting to become what others want us to be.

In redemption-based spirituality, we ask the question and God provides the answer. In creation-centered spirituality, God asks the question and we are the answer.

These somewhat opposing views have had a significant impact on the lives of everyone, whether they had direct early experiences with a religion or only grew up in a society dominated by religious ideas. The fields of education, religion, psychology, sociology, and politics must ultimately address these important issues. Denying or reacting against religions will not help; such actions only serve to fixate the person's energy all the more, creating more walls and resistances that produce more blocks. Many people drop out of formal religions, often seeking some other expression of their spirituality. In North America, where alternative life-styles have become de rigueur, people are drawn toward eastern religions, which often offer the promise of liberation and ultimate answers. Too often, ironically, the very people who are attempting to escape from the tyranny of authoritarian rule will submit to the authority of a guru or another form of religion (such as some New Age leader) in the hope of finding enlightenment or absolute truths.

In creation-centered spirituality, the authority for meaning remains centered in the Self. Alternative meanings or even opposing points of view can be considered, sorted, and digested, but should never be swallowed whole or taken on as "the truth." Each person (being God) is considered to be whole, capable of discovering a personal meaning or truth from within. Sometimes advocates of this position unwittingly adopt an isolationist perspective, forgetting that this point of view recognizes the God within every person, which is the same God for everyone, thus connecting us all. Our task is not to become God, or to fashion the Self to please God, but rather to *discover* God (the elements of meaning of the Self) within. As an expression of a structuralist philosophy, creation-centered spirituality would have us discover the patterns of existence (God) in any of our levels of being—in our bodies, our feelings, our minds, and our relationships.

> *To love another person is to see the face of God.*
> —from the musical *Les Misérables* by Andrew Lloyd Webber

Redemption-centered spirituality assumes that we are born imperfect or incomplete (in sin) and that we need to make reparations and submit to a higher power to become perfect. In creation-centered spirituality each person is believed to be whole, connected to all others and the universe, as part of a total energy flow; however, because of a limited state of consciousness, the experience of being connected is lost; sin is the state of being *unaware* of that connection. The goal of this kind of spirituality is to rediscover that connection, reaffirming the wholeness of existence through self-awareness and raising the level of consciousness; the authority remains within the person, not in others or in outside structures or institutions. Creation-centered spirituality is self-centered but is not selfish, self-indulgent, or self-promoting. It assumes that God is expressed in all of life's experiences, including those that appear to be negative, dark, and frightening.

Redemption-centered spirituality, found in both eastern and western religions, offers redemption or enlightenment through renunciation, atonement, self-denial, or disengagement from the material, physical world; salvation offers relief from guilt, pain, and suffering. Spiritual practices in redemption-centered spirituality are *transcendental* in nature, through self-denial, self-punishment, or disengagement from the Self. On the other hand, creation-centered spirituality emphasizes living more fully in the present, acknowledging all aspects (both dark and light) of the Self, becoming more self-aware, with a higher level of consciousness. Learning through relating is one of the *transformational* approaches; discovering creative expression of all sides of the Self is one of the goals. Spirituality is experienced at all levels of being, at all times. God is expressed in each man and woman being fully alive, as free of fixations as possible, willing to allow the energy flow into all niches of experience, without bias or prejudice. Creation-centered spirituality acknowledges a oneness, with responsibility (response-ability) but not license. In eastern religions this is the "every-minute Zen" philosophy of being fully present and fully aware. Because God is assumed to be ever-present in all things, the discovery of God requires a mindfulness and awareness, rather than a striving toward perfection.

God's being is my being
 and God's primordial being
is my primordial being.

Wherever I am,
 there is God.
The eye with which I see God
 is the same eye with which God sees me.[2]

—Meister Eckhart

Notes
1. M. Fox, *Meditations with Meister Eckhart* (Santa Fe: Bear and Company, 1983), 5.
2. Ibid., 20-21.

Recommended Reading
Fox, M. *Original Blessing*. Santa Fe, NM: Bear & Co., 1983.

DISTINCTIONS

This section contains a number of paired concepts that are often confused with each other. Avoid the ready trap of seeing the following concepts in moralistic terms. In considering these issues, do not feel obliged to choose one of the paired concepts as "right" or "true" and therefore "better" than the other. Instead, the process of *discernment* involves seeing the concepts for what they are and investigating your own perspective on them.

MORALITY AND PERSONAL ETHICS

The moral code of "appropriateness," "rightness," and "truth" is very useful as an organizing principle in maintaining a social order. However, society with its requirements often fails to consider the needs and concerns of the individual. In fitting in, one often loses the ability to think for oneself. Abiding by the moral code without question serves to reduce existential anxiety, the terror of being. But reducing anxiety also reduces life, and the spontaneous creativity of the individual is gradually stifled. In this trade, the person has the security of fitting in; however, individual freedom is severely reduced by shackling the mind. Morality involves the duality of right/wrong. In a moral position, certain values and actions are judged "correct," "true," or "right" and others are judged to be "incorrect," "false," or "wrong." From a nonmoral position, nothing is ever right or wrong; rather, different situations demand careful scrutiny to determine one's own personal position, determined by one's own value system.

The issue of discernment is very important for the development of the individual Self. To discover one's personal perspective on key issues, it is necessary to relinquish the footholds of conventional moral thinking and "free fall" into the chaos of unstructured concepts. Discernment does not mean abandoning society's moral guidelines, but it does mean thinking for oneself, rather than swallowing, without consideration, the predigested perspectives of the culture at large. To unthinkingly adopt the attitudes dictated by society is to accept a conventional morality; when one applies discernment to make distinctions and arrive at one's personal standpoint, this is the action of personal ethics (see above, "Morality").

RESPONSIBILITY AND BLAME

It is a common misconception that responsibility and blame are the same. To be responsible is to hold one's Self accountable for participating in any action, either voluntarily or involuntarily, consciously or unconsciously. If a pedestrian is accidentally struck by a car while crossing a street, that person is responsible for being the one crossing the street, perhaps not being fully mindful of the circumstances, perhaps even being in a self-destructive state. From the framework of responsibility, both the driver and the pedestrian have a story to tell that reveals each person's participation in the accident.

The framework of blame presupposes a morality of right and wrong; some person is at fault. The focus of attention is on weighing the evidence to discover which of the parties is at fault and which one is the victim; who is guilty and who is innocent. From childhood onward, much of a person's experience is framed in these terms, so it is difficult to step outside this grid and view experience from a morality-free framework.

To take the example of infectious diseases, the person is usually seen to be the victim of germs, which are considered to be the perpetrators of the illness. In the framework of responsibility, the ill person is considered to be responsible for creating the circumstances in which the germs grew, and for the state of the body's vulnerability to that particular organism. The illness process need not be seen in light of good or bad; it is seen as a manifestation of a great number of processes in which the ill person has participated, consciously or unconsciously, at some level of being. Nothing and nobody is at fault; each has a responsibility for participation in the event, each with a story to tell, with individual purposes to be served.

The holistic health movement rests squarely on the concept of individual responsibility for states of health and illness. There are no victims, but at the same time, nobody or nothing is seen as at fault. The focus is on the individual's participation in the illness process from beginning to end, on the purposes that are served by such participation, on the story that is being told, and on the metaphor that is unfolding.

In the concepts of complementary medicine, although traditional methods of treatment are being applied to the illness process, attention is given to helping the person discover the reasons for creating, participating in, or supporting the illness. Unfortunately, many subscribers to holistic health become hostile to what traditional medicine can offer in the way of help; they sometimes even blame the person (sometimes themselves!) suffering from the illness. This guilt-producing attitude contributes to the perpetuation of the illness rather than furthering the healing process.

GUILT AND SHAME

Guilt is the feeling of discomfort and tension that is experienced by a person who has broken some imposed rule or law for which that individual has some respect. Guilt is always related to some external judgment, some morality that has been internalized so that the external source need not even be present at the time of the infraction. The bodily reaction in guilt is to tighten up, close down, feel cold, and develop a state of tension. The person feels caught, trapped, and in danger of being punished. Neurophysiologically, the experience is primarily sympathetic (a reaction of the autonomic nervous system) in nature. It is the Self in danger of consequences for not living up to the expectations of others. Existentially, it is a nonbeing state.

Shame arises as a feeling only in reference to the Self, not to external sources, as with guilt. The person recognizes an exposure of the Actual self that falls short of what it believes it can really be, or what it is truly capable of doing. Thus, shame is always related to self-recognition, awareness of one's own expectations and the image of one's Self. The bodily reaction is one of flushing, of filling up with warmth, of being exposed and naked, and of being without defense. Neurophysiologically, the experience is primarily parasympathetic in nature. It is the Self recognizing the Self, in danger of being revealed when it doesn't desire to be so, and wishing to hide. Existentially, it is a being state (as described above in "Perspectives on Guilt and Shame").

FAITH AND HOPE

Faith is the felt sense of the assurance of the continuity of life. It involves a sense of confidence in meaning without requiring a rational or logical explanation; it is experienced at a level deeper than the intellectual, relating to a profound sense of trust without supporting evidence. Existentially, it is a being state with a recognition of, but not a fear of, the nonbeing state.

Hope is always related to expectations for the future that will satisfy some unfulfilled desire or wish in the present. The promise of fulfilling those desires may tie the person to some external authority or force, and frequently excuses the Self from having to take responsibility in the present. So, essentially hope involves a denial or lack of acceptance of the present; in this way, hope is a moving away from life. Existentially, it is primarily a nonbeing state anticipating a future improvement.

SURRENDER AND SUBMISSION

These terms become very confusing in relation to sexuality; they also are involved in nonsexual interactions. People seem to arrive at a belief that love can be expressed in its highest form through the act of surrender. At the same time, they are warned against becoming dominated by somebody else (as could be inferred in the act of surrender) for fear of losing their own identity. This dilemma can best be untangled through an understanding of the difference between surrender and submission.

The act of submission is related to power. One person places the Self at the disposal of another, to yield or to give over to the other. *The main referent is the other*; the Self is diminished in importance. However, as in all power circumstances, both the dominator and submitter are invested with control of the other, albeit from seemingly opposite ends of the pole. In existential terms, the exciting charge that is experienced over the prospect of submission is related to the flirtation with nonexistence or death, the giving up (or the taking over) of all responsibility through the ultimate dissolution of the will.

The act of surrender is related to giving up of control of the Self, and its *referent is only to the Self*, not to another. In order to survive and be rewarded in society, each person needs to develop control over the Self (self-control) through roles, social conventions and task competency. Such self-restraint is important to the development of one's personality, but at the same time it inhibits spontaneity and involves some loss of sense of Self. The act of giving up such controls (as in surrender) results in a feeling of letting go, an exhilaration, a sense of experiencing one's Self again, fresh and recognizable. The Self is increased in importance and strength and is known to itself in a deeper way.

All relationships involve a dance between submission and surrender of the people involved, with alternating development of personal strength (as with surrender) and power (as with submission/domination). The relative amounts of those experiences determine the nature of a relationship and the possibility for personal growth within it.

POWER AND STRENGTH

Power involves ability to exert control and ascendance over another, and a position of dominance. On the other hand, strength is related to the solidity of the Self, independent of the other. Thus, power is always related to an object or person that is external to the Self (or to the "Self as object," which involves a process of depersonalization), whereas strength is related only to the quality of endurance of the Self, unrelated to the other. A person with strength requires less power, because the person is self-sufficient.

Every experience offers opportunities for exercising either strength (as with risk-taking and vulnerability) or power (as with moral and political events). Most relationships are governed by power politics, with strong needs for each individual to be "right." Sharing feelings, revealing each person's view of the world, and being vulnerable one to the other allow each person to grow in strength. (For further discussion see above, "Strength and Power").

FEAR AND EXCITEMENT

The physiological responses to fear and excitement are similar, perhaps even identical. The heart rate quickens, breathing is increased, the skin perspires and perhaps develops "goose-pimples," the hair seems to lift, the pupils of the eyes enlarge. These symptoms of the "fight or flight" syndrome are the same, whether the person is in danger of being beaten up or is experiencing an imminent possibility of winning a million dollars in a lottery!

The only difference between such experiences is the person's judgment of the situation. With excitement the person wants to be present in the danger-producing experience (as in a roller-coaster); when the person has not freely chosen to be there, and danger is threatening, the person interprets the experience as fear. Frequently, but not always, the person has the belief that ultimately, in exciting situations safety has been provided; where that safety is not perceived, the person usually will interpret their feeling as fear instead of excitement.

CYNICISM AND IRONY

Cynicism involves a putting down of experience and a stepping back from life. The contempt for life in cynicism is self-defeating and involves pride and presumption (as if the cynic actually knows what is best, looking down on the world). Cynicism often accompanies the lack of courage to face life as it is. The contemptuous cynic disapproves of life rather than entering it.

Irony involves a very intimate appreciation and acceptance of life. Irony is a very high form of humor, which acknowledges life as it is. There is humility associated with irony (contrasted with the pride associated with cynicism).

SACRED AND HOLY

"Sacred" is an adjective used to describe situations that have been elevated to the status of special, important, honored, inviolate, separate, and better. Involved in the usage of the term "sacred" is a morality, which elevates what is sacred; we make "sacred ground" and "sacred cows," and then do battle to conserve them. In this way, to make something sacred is to separate that item from the rest of life.

"Holy" involves a joining to life. When experiencing the holy, a person participates in a responsive manner. To appreciate each circumstance as connected to all of life is to have a "holistic" (*holos*—"whole") viewpoint and a participation in the holy. A person experiences the holy aspect of any situation when its relationship to the rest of life is recognized and felt. Unlike the sacred, there is nothing special about the holy; in *every* situation, a person participates in the holy, but does not always appreciate it.

> *The wretchedness of our world is grounded in its resistance to the entrance of the holy into lived life.*[1]
>
> —Martin Buber

PERFECTION AND EXCELLENCE

Perfection is related to the Ideal self, and involves striving, achievement, and denial of the Authentic Self. As outlined above (see "The Ideal Self: Striving

For Perfection"), seeking perfection is associated with self-hatred and dissatisfaction with life. Thus, perfection is related to nonbeing.

Excellence is a function of the Authentic Self and is related to mastery. Excellence involves an acceptance of life, not a striving for perfection but rather a standing forth in expressing one's potential. Excellence comes with self-realization and self-expression. It is an attribute of being.

MINIMALISM AND MINIMIZATION

Minimalism is a philosophy of doing just enough, reflecting a sensitive relationship with life and an appreciation of it. To minimize is to devalue something, diminishing its importance. Minimizing acts against life by not accepting it. Minimalism is a life-enhancing attitude, involving only the appropriate use of resources and no waste.

PRESENCE AND INTIMACY

Presence involves being in the here and now. Intimacy involves a revelation and a sharing of the Self. One can be present and not intimate; when one is intimate, one is also present.

PARODY AND MOCKERY

To parody someone is to know them intimately and then humorously represent aspects of their character; often, parody involves a sensitive appreciation and love for the person and may be accompanied by a closeness or a joining.

Mockery is a put-down that involves contempt and derision. Often, mockery is used in the service of power and dominance over the other.

ALONENESS AND LONELINESS/ISOLATION

Aloneness is a condition of human existence that involves apartness and uniqueness. It is neither positive nor negative; it is just a given. Acceptance of aloneness permits people to feel their deepest nature. Loneliness is experienced when a person does not accept aloneness, believing that existence can be different. Such a person walls off from the world, feeling self-pity for not having a companion. Ironically, a person becomes closest to others by accepting that (s)he is alone. The feeling of isolation is most acute when a person does not accept that all other people cannot alter the essential separateness of the Self. Aloneness involves self-reliance; loneliness arises in field dependence.

ANGER AND VIOLENCE

Anger is a feeling that arises when love is frustrated and connection is interrupted. First the person is liable to feel hurt or frightened, uncovering an underlying feeling of helplessness; the anger arises to move the person out of that helplessness. It results from a great variety of situations, such as unmet expectations, crossed boundaries, and devalued self-esteem. As such, anger is neither negative nor positive; it is merely a feeling response on the part of the individual. When anger is shared, it can enhance intimacy (as can any internal state that is shared).

Violence is the act of crossing boundaries without permission. Thus, the key to violence is consent: with consent there is no violence, regardless of the act. It is even possible to perpetrate violence with love, or in the name of love, if boundaries are crossed without consent. When anger is shared with permission and within clearly defined and agreed upon limits, it is not violence.

REBELLION AND STANDING FORTH

Rebellion occurs when one acts against another; there is a defiance and a field dependency associated with rebellion. In this reaction against something or somebody, one becomes tied and dependent upon that something or somebody. With rebellion or revolution, individuality and independence are attained.

Standing forth occurs when one firmly asserts oneself. This is not done against anyone else; rather, it is an affirmation and expression of the Self, quite independent of the other. This process is one of growth, which provides for the development of autonomy and individuation.

SUMMARY

The above list contains important but confusing concepts that require some attention. By clarifying these, it is possible for people to locate themselves in life in a way that frees them from the tyranny of moral injunctions. Furthermore, clarifying the meanings of these concepts will facilitate communication with others so that more intimacy can be enjoyed. Responsibility and personal growth are then possible without the need to rebel against a society that intends to help, but all too often only hinders individual development.

Notes
1. M. Buber, *Hasidism and Modern Man*, edited & translated by Maurice Friedman (New York: Harper Torchbooks, 1966), 180.

EPILOGUE

Dear Reader:

If you have been able to persevere to the end of the Manual, you will have a general idea of some of our basic assumptions about life, relationships and the exigencies of human nature. By now, you will have probably discovered that in developing these ideas, we have borrowed extensively from a wide variety of sources. Furthermore, these ideas have been tried and tempered through our interactions with the thousands of people who have graced us with their presence. To all of those—participants, thinkers, scientists, theologians, authors, professionals, seekers, etc.—we express our deepest gratitude.

We agree with the eastern philosophers and some existentialists who posit that the human being is suspended somewhere between the earth and heaven, facing the need to survive while yearning for a felt sense of meaning, some reason to survive. Since survival needs seem best to be served through co-operation and organization, each individual frequently finds the demands of the self at odds with the demands of society and culture. Individual development reflects that dynamic tension. Most often, the self is sacrificed for conformity and security; however, the inner yearning for fuller expression of that self cannot be completely extinguished. Throughout history, many different kinds of political systems have come up against that irrepressible desire for freedom of expression of the self.

When the self cannot be fully expressed, the cost is enormous, although often subtle and disguised. These disguises may take on a wide range of symptom formations at all levels of being—emotional, spiritual, mental and physical. At root there is a common thread of isolation and anxiety resulting from a separation not only from others, but more fundamentally, a separation from the self! It is our observation that much of human endeavor is aimed towards healing those separations; it is also our experience that most people lack many of the basic tools to effect such a healing. Instead of exercising personal responsibility, many people tend to ascribe power and authority to others.

We fervently wish that this Manual has been able to provide you with some of the understanding and tools that can be used to heal your own personal rifts, and has contributed to the development of some faith in yourself.

You are not alone!

Jock McKeen & Bennet Wong
Gabriola Island, B.C., October, 1992

INDEX

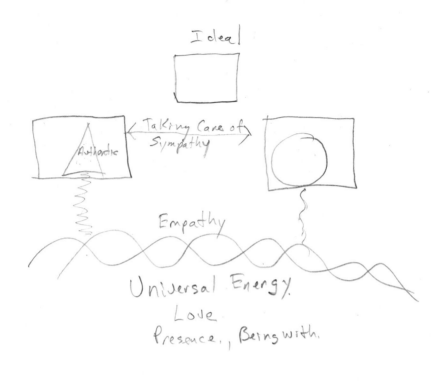

Ideal

Taking Care of
Sympathy

Authentic

Empathy

Universal Energy.
Love.
Presence., Being with.